ON TAXES
AND INFLATION

STUDIES

IN ECONOMICS

Consulting Editor:

WILLIAM LETWIN

Massachusetts Institute of Technology

On Taxes and Inflation

AMOTZ MORAG

The Hebrew University, Jerusalem, Israel

RANDOM HOUSE · NEW YORK

FIRST PRINTING

© Copyright, 1965, by Random House, Inc.

All rights reserved under International and Pan-American Copyright Conventions. Published in New York by Random House, Inc., and simultaneously in Toronto, Canada, by Random House of Canada, Limited.

Library of Congress Catalog Card Number: 64-24764

Composition by ELECTRA COMPOSITION CORP., New York
Printed and bound by H. WOLFF BOOK MFG. CO., New York

TO
THE MEMORY OF
MY FATHER

Preface

THIS SMALL BOOK makes no pretensions of being a treatise. In many ways, it is simply a collection of essays connected by the personality of their author and by a personal outlook on the subject of taxes and inflation. This outlook is characterized by a strong stress on monetary factors in tax analysis, by an approach to tax incidence based on changes in the *relative* prices of products and of factors of production, and by special attention to the psychological costs of taxation.

As the reader will note, my outlook is influenced, much beyond what the footnotes convey, by the contributions of Richard A. Musgrave and Don Patinkin. While the incidence analysis in this study only draws out some new implications of Musgrave's approach, I have not followed him in other respects: for instance, my expressed interest in minimizing the psychological costs of taxation differs from his stand on this issue. One's attitude here should indeed depend on his own evaluation of the optimal size of the budget in relation to its actual size at a given time and place. The arguments presented here for hidden taxes may indeed be turned against them if illusions of costless public services do invite uneconomic public expenditures.

Some of the material in this book is based on articles which have already been published in journals: Chapter 1 on an article which appeared in *Public Finance*, Vol. XIV, No. 1 (1959); Chapter 3 on articles published in *The Economic Journal*, Vol. LXIX

(March 1959), and in *The Journal of Political Economy*, Vol. LXVII, No. 3 (June 1959); and Chapter 4 on an article published in *The National Tax Journal*, Vol. XI, No. 3 (September 1958). A section of Chapter 6 is based on an article which appeared in *The American Economic Review*, Vol. LII, No. 1 (March 1962). I am indebted to all these journals for permission to republish here parts of those articles.

In spite of the brevity of this book, the list of those from whose advice this study has benefited is very long. The intellectual debt to Patinkin and Musgrave has already been mentioned. And in addition to the influence of Musgrave's published works, many ideas presented here also stem from lectures and discussions in his Public Finance Seminar and in the General Seminar in Economics at Johns Hopkins University where I was a post-doctoral fellow in 1960/61. I wish also to thank the various members of the Johns Hopkins faculty and graduate-student body for many stimulating comments. Among my colleagues in Jerusalem, with whom I discussed several points intensively, I must include especially Messrs. Yossef Attiyeh, Nissan Liviatan, Michael Michaely, Tsvi Ophir, and A. Sheshinsky. Professor Fritz Machlup had, perhaps unknowingly, much to do with this study, for many ideas presented here are an outgrowth of my Ph.D. dissertation prepared under his loving guidance.

The post-doctoral year during which I wrote most of this study was made possible by a grant from the Ford Foundation for which, naturally, I am most thankful. More than that, due to special circumstances, I had an opportunity to benefit from the personal generosity of the administrators of the Ford Foundation and of the Institute of International Education.

AMOTZ MORAG

The Hebrew University
Jerusalem, Israel

CONTENTS

ONE   THE LIMITS OF TAXATION   3

Defining the Limits of Taxation   5
Why Taxes May Reach a Limit   15

TWO   TAXES, MONEY, AND PRICES   24

Why Indirect Taxes Raise the Price Level   28
The Location of Taxes and the Price Level   33
Shifting and Attempted Shifting   35

THREE   THE DEFLATIONARY EFFECTS
OF TAXES   46

Is the Economic Efficiency of Taxes
Important?   49
Deflationary Effects of Outlay Taxes
and Income Taxes   58

FOUR   ON PROGRESSIVE TAXATION   73

The Time Dimension of Progressivity   75
Partial Progressivity   79
Progressivity, Progression, and "Morals"   87

FIVE   TAXES AND THE SUPPLY OF
RESOURCES   94

Effects on Labor Supply   96

Effects on Saving and Investment 98
Taxation and Risk-Taking 102
Conclusions 110

SIX ON INDIRECTNESS IN TAXATION 114

The Case for Indirect Income Taxes 127

SEVEN INFLATION AS A TAX 142

Deficit Financing 149
Toward an Inflation-proof Economy 154
Escalation and Ordinary Taxes 169

INDEX 177

ON TAXES
AND INFLATION

CHAPTER ONE

THE LIMITS
OF TAXATION

It is a common belief that there must be a limit to the level of taxation. Even most of the numerous economists who tend to reject the thesis, submitted by Colin Clark in several articles,[1] that taxable capacity cannot exceed a quarter of national income, criticize mainly his statistical demonstration. The very idea that taxes must have some limits tends to be thought of as obvious because the base for all taxes is clearly limited by the size of G.N.P. and National Wealth. Consequently, any new thesis about limits to taxation must be stated in a form of the limits being at some percentage of the national income or of the net national product or of the gross national product, or whatever is argued by the submitter of a new thesis, which thus necessarily must be a statistical thesis.

But paradoxically, statistics can neither prove nor disprove such a thesis. In this connection, Clark argues that passing through the "natural" limit of taxation will always bring about inflation. But even if this is true —and this will be much discussed in this study—it certainly would not be the first of the hardships brought about by taxes. Nor is it certain that the hardships of inflation would always necessarily exceed the benefits of marginal public expenditures.

But disregarding such doubts, it should be made clear at the beginning that even if a very high positive correlation were found between time series of taxes as percentages of, say, net national product, and indices of price level, it would not be at all clear whether any direct causality obtained between the two series, and if there did, which way it went. Indeed, a rise in prices may be the result of increases in the rates of some taxes. But to the extent that the price rise is not tax-induced it will, should the tax system be at all progressive, raise the real value of the taxes collected and their *ratio* to national income. Correspondingly, a lack of significant statistical relationships between the two statistical series does not abolish possibilities of lagged influences. Colin Clark himself expressed despair of the statistical method which can never prove a case of causality. Certainly it is strange that, in spite of his own emphasis on such socio-political factors as inflationary and deflationary pressure groups, Clark arrived at a conclusion that the limits of taxation are the same, or at least almost the same, in such countries as the United Kingdom, the United States, Italy, Japan, France, Belgium, and Norway.

It would be astonishing if the relative strength of the inflationary and deflationary pressure-groups were that similar in all these countries. Indeed, if the size of taxable capacity does have something to do with the burden of servicing the national debt, with the size and/or distribution of national income either between income groups or between wages, rents, interest payments, and profits, with the relative strength of labor unions, with monetary policies, with the kinds of taxes in use and with their effect on the distribution of income, with the efficiency of the tax administration and with the morale of the taxpayers, with conditions of the balance of payments, with past experiences of inflation, and with what not—then it would be truly amazing were taxable capacity still the same size everywhere, or almost everywhere. One does not have to be an institutionalist to admit that economic forces do not work in a vacuum, so that, *a priori,* their effects are not likely to be quantitatively the same, regardless of the kind of economy involved, even if the forces themselves are identical, which they cannot be.

Thus, if Clark's contention that taxable capacity is about 25 per cent of national income is rejected—not because of a belief that it is higher or lower, but because one takes for granted that the limits of taxation are probably quite different in each economy—all that remains of his thesis is that there are limits to taxation.

DEFINING THE LIMITS OF TAXATION

Capacity is not exactly an economic term. Indeed, economists rarely discuss the capacity of firms or of industries. For a layman the capacity of a firm seems to be reached when the firm cannot produce any more, that is, when the marginal physical output of additional variable factors of production is zero, if not negative. But in a world of economic scarcity such output would not and should not be produced. The economic question is how much the firm should produce—that is, what is its optimum output, not what is its maximum output, and the answer to this question changes with economic conditions. The same distinction between possibility and desirability holds when taxable capacity is discussed.

For if the problem is how much taxes a government can possibly impose, the answer, since taxes are paid compulsorily, must be: 100 per cent of national income plus taxation in kind (once for all) of all the privately-held national wealth. Citizens would not necessarily starve even if taxation did reach such heights, for nothing is stated about the nature of government expenditures; they might be mainly transfer payments. There remains, of course, the problem of incentives and certainly, it is quite likely that a government imposing that much in taxes, or even less, would be angrily overthrown by the public. Even more likely, an economy from which so much taxes were squeezed would probably stop being a free economy. But these important questions of the political capacity of taxation belong properly within the realm of the political scientist or sociologist. The question for the nonpolitical economist is how many taxes should a government impose, that is, what is the economic capacity of taxation?

The orthodox answer to this question used to be that, since a budget should always be balanced, the level of taxation is determined by the level of government expenditures. The neo-orthodox answer, that of the Functional Finance school, is that the level of taxation should be determined so as to achieve full employment and a stable price level. Both answers imply that economic taxable capacity as such does not exist, as is made very clear by Abba P. Lerner's criticism of the opponents of Functional Finance. Lerner argues that if taxes imposed to prevent inflation according to the rules of Functional Finance do not result in proceeds sufficient to finance total government expenditures, including the servicing of the debt, then the "interest on the debt can be met by borrowing or printing the money. There is no risk of inflation from this, *because if there were such a risk a greater amount would have to be collected in taxes*".[2] That is, the government can and should impose as much taxes as the rules of Functional Finance dictate. With full employment in the economy this means as much taxes as are needed to finance government expenditures. In short, there is no taxable capacity.

Yet while it is clear that government expenditures do have to be financed, the problems of the level of government expenditures and the level of taxation are not identical. Ideally, government expenditures should be increased up to the point where the marginal social benefits of a dollar of expenditure (either on the supply of public consumption, or on transfer payments, or on public investment) equal the marginal social sacrifices imposed on the economy by the additional expenditure. While the magnitudes of the marginal social benefits and marginal social sacrifices are not measurable, this definition of the economic *capacity of government expenditures* seems to be conceptually clear. The size of the capacity of government expenditures may perhaps be approximated "by comparing the real product of the economic system with that part of it which is needed for the satisfaction of indispensable needs, exclusive of those rendered by the Government".[3] Kuznets argues that this could be a conceivable method of measuring taxable capacity, which must have been defined by him as the capacity of government expenditures.

However, once the optimal size of government expenditures is decided upon, the problem of *how* to finance it still remains unanswered. A government can finance its expenditures by various taxes, or by borrowing from abroad, or from the public, or from the commercial banks, or from the central bank, or, if this is institutionally allowed, by printing its own money.

One choice to be made is between taxation and inflation. Taxation, to be sure, is superior to inflation, but this superiority is not really the point. The economic choice is always at the margin and it is conceivable that at a certain level of taxation the marginal social sacrifice of some deficit financing would be lower than the marginal social sacrifice of further taxation. This is usually the case when the economy is underemployed, since the marginal social sacrifices of deficit financing are quite low and may even be negative if indirect "multiplier benefits" are deducted from them. But even when deficit financing means inflation, the social costs of *some* inflationary deficit financing and *more* taxation should always be compared. Inflationary deficit financing is also a tax, and it should be considered and used just like any other tax when it is less costly at the margin than other taxes available.

A rational government will always use first the means of finance that involve the lowest marginal social costs. That is, tax with the lowest of such costs will be among the first to be implemented. When this first tax reaches a certain level of revenues, however, the marginal social costs of its further use may begin to exceed those of another. This is where the first tax reaches its capacity. Assuming that the marginal social costs of each tax depend only on the size of governmental revenues, further revenues will then be raised by a second tax until it, too, reaches its capacity—that is, when its marginal social costs exceed those of a third tax. And so it goes, through a series of taxes. This is probably the main reason why the meaning of a "better tax" is so ambiguous. Thus an income tax may seem to be much better than, say, an excise on sugar, but an increase in an income tax is not necessarily "better" than the imposition of that excise. This is also the reason why the only case in which a Henry Georgian single-tax idea would be justified, and one tax be given a "fiscal monopoly," is where the marginal social cost curve of this tax did not intersect from below a marginal cost curve of any other tax (or, if it did, the intersection would have to take place where the proceeds from this first and only tax exceeded the revenue requirements of the government).

Taxation in its ordinary sense will reach its capacity when—and this might happen—the marginal costs of a certain tax exceed the costs of borrowings, in which case the wise decision would be: no more taxes. The same process applies, of course, to the different kinds of borrowings, so that borrowing from the public will reach its limits when the wise decision is to stop borrowing, and so on. Naturally, a government has to make many financial decisions; attention here will be paid mainly to the choice between tax finance and borrowing from the banking system and especially from the central bank (if institutionally feasible).

Figure 1 represents diagrammatically the argument that taxable capacity is reached when further taxation is socially more costly, at the margin, than deficit financing.

Figure 1 reflects the assumption that the marginal social costs of each tax at each level of government revenues are a function only of the size of government revenues and would be the same, therefore, whether all revenues up to that point were raised by this tax itself or by other taxes. The first tax is the source of OA of government revenues, the second of AC, the third of CD. But when government expenditures necessitate a revenue bigger than OD, deficit financing has to be used to finance any additional expenditure, since at the margin it is less costly.

The assumption underlying Figure 1 is clearly unrealistic. Certainly the marginal costs of, say, the "second tax" at point S would be different were the first *OA* dollars of government expenditures financed by the first tax, by the second tax itself, or by any other tax. A diametrically opposite assumption could be that the level of revenues from each tax, and not the level of all government revenues, determines the marginal social costs of each tax. Figure 2 depicts the process of reaching taxable capacity according to this second assumption.

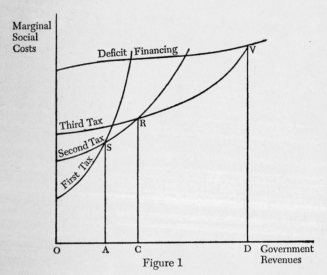

Figure 1

In Figure 2 the government will use the first tax exclusively as long as its needs for revenues do not exceed *BA*. After this stage an increase in expenditures will be financed simultaneously by both the first and the second tax, equalizing the marginal costs of the two taxes. The third tax will be imposed when the revenue needs are higher than $BA + AN + BV$, continuously applying the rule of equalizing marginal costs. If this is not sufficient, another tax will be introduced, and so on, until the relatively efficient source of additional finance is not a tax at all, as ordinarily defined. Graphically, given the optimal size of the government budget, it would be quite simple to allocate the revenues among the various taxes, the marginal social costs of which are horizontally aggregated.

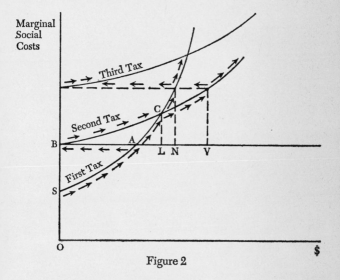

Figure 2

Figure 3 illustrates this point for the case of two methods of finance, the marginal social costs of which are assumed, for the sake of simplicity, to be linear. AD is the optimal size of the government budget, with $EKDL$ signifying the marginal social costs of finance; it is a horizontal sum of EF, the marginal social cost of the first method of finance and GH, the marginal social cost of the second. Out of *AD*, the amount of finance needed, *AC* is collected through the first method, while *AB* (= *CD*) is collected through the second.

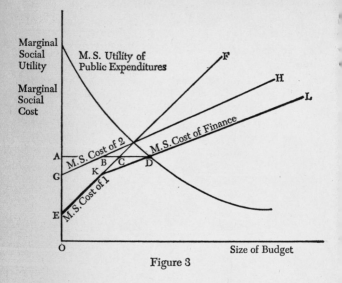

Figure 3

Although the process depicted in Figures 2 and 3 is probably more true to life, the assumption underlying it is even less realistic than that of Figure 1. Obviously the social costs of a specific tax are a function of both total government revenues and of the revenues of that tax and of other factors, like the structure of the tax and its relative rates.

To repeat, taxable capacity is reached when the marginal social costs of further taxation exceed those of alternative sources. Like any definition, this one is somewhat arbitrary. Colin Clark himself does not explicitly define taxable capacity. But if I interpret his arguments correctly, his implicit definition of taxable capacity is that level of taxation where the marginal taxes reduce private spending by less than they reduce output, and thus are actually more inflationary than deficit financing.[4] Such a level of taxation is possible but it is hard to understand why taxation should be carried that far. Certainly the marginal social costs of taxes would exceed those of deficit financing much before this stage since, after all, deficits are less painful than ordinary taxes.

The rather technical definition of taxable capacity —as the amount of tax revenues where the marginal social costs of taxation start to exceed the curve of the marginal costs of any other source of finance—does not, of course, help one to understand why such a point should exist. That it often does is empirically obvious. Thus Clark and his critics alike omit the World War II years from their statistics, probably because Clark would admit that taxable capacity—as implicitly defined by him—is probably higher than normal during wartime because of a greater readiness to pay taxes. A greater willingness to pay taxes, it will be noted, might also increase taxable capacity as defined here, by lowering the marginal social costs of taxation at all levels of taxation. The psychological disutility of paying taxes is undoubtedly an important part of the social costs of taxation. To include the war years in the time series might perhaps weaken the claim that taxable capacity is 25 per cent of national income, but certainly it would support the more fundamental claim that taxable capacity as defined here is a "practical" concept. For just as it was a major instrument of finance during the Great Depression, deficit financing has also been widely used in war years in most countries.[5]

The use of deficit financing in a depression is self-explanatory: at such times, taxable capacity is extremely low because the marginal social costs of deficit finance are very low (if positive). Wars also are generally associated with deficit—and in this case inflationary—financing. In this instance, however, the *why* is not at all obvious. The argument that governments need "money" immediately during wars and that tax administrations are not usually well prepared for such emergencies cannot explain the continuous and often *increasing* use of deficit financing during long wars. The argument that it is impossible to finance the vast war expenditures by taxation is obviously false, and smacks of the "physical" meaning of taxable capacity. According to the estimates of William J. Fellner it would have been possible to prevent any inflationary potential in the U.S. during the war years by an additional proportional income tax of 10 per cent.[6] Whether this should or should not have been done is debatable, but certainly it could have been done. Then there are arguments that in emergency situations the government must bid up the prices of the resources it needs. During a war, so runs the argument, victory comes first, and nothing should be done to discourage incentives to economic activity. In short, no high taxes.

But the question is not whether increases in some prices should be allowed during mobilization and war. Unless artificially forbidden they will take place —whatever the methods of finance used—because of the increase in government expenditures. It also remains to be proved that inflation (of all kinds) necessarily discourages incentives to economic activity less than taxes do. Indeed, it is not even clear that all taxes necessarily do that. But, in any case, all that is implied in these arguments is that the marginal social costs of taxation are higher during wartimes since the "social value" of every additional output is that high. Thus taxable capacity during wartime might, in spite of the greater readiness to pay taxes which works in the opposite direction, be *lower* than normal.

Taxable capacity is thus a very "practical" concept, and not only in times of war. The problem of whether development should be financed, partly or wholly, by deficit financing, also revolves mainly on differing implicit views on the size of taxable capacity.

WHY TAXES MAY REACH A LIMIT

That taxation may reach capacity is quite clear, but it is not so clear why. The concept of taxable capacity is based on an assumption that the marginal costs of taxation rise; for if they were constant (not to say decreasing) they could hardly be expected to exceed those of deficit financing and inflation at any level of taxation. Thus it is important to examine if the marginal social costs of taxation do indeed rise, and if so, why?

The costs of taxation are determined by its effects, the latter of which might be divided into three categories: 1) income, or purchasing-power, effects, 2) distributional effects, and 3) allocational or the so-called "announcement effects."[7] To be sure, these three effects of taxation are interconnected, but for the moment we shall treat them as if they were not. The term "announcement effect" is unfortunate since such effects have very little to do with the effects of new taxes as contrasted with those of old. Pigou chose the term to denote its dependency on "the scheme of formulae in which their own liability is *announced* to each taxpayer."[8] Such effects, it has been explained, "arise from the presence of a positive rate of tax upon a base subject to greater or less control by the taxpayer."[9]

At first, one tends to treat the problem of taxable capacity in terms of the income effects of taxation. Since the marginal utility of disposable income rises with a decrease in disposable income, the marginal disutility of paying taxes increases with the level of taxation. This alone would suffice to explain why the curve of the marginal social costs of taxation rises, and therefore why it must eventually intersect the declining curve of the marginal social benefits of government expenditure. But it cannot help us to understand why there is more than one tax in the fiscal system and why taxes might reach their capacity. For, abstracting from distributional effects, the social disutility of paying taxes presented by their purchasing-power effects is determined exclusively by the size of government expenditures. It is therefore better to speak of the real disposable income effects of government expenditures rather than those of taxes. These effects can therefore explain why the first but not why the latter might reach capacity.

Were the purchasing-power effects the only ones that mattered, inflation would do just as well as taxation as a method of government finance. Indeed, if the government could print money or borrow without limits from the banking system, the main purpose of ordinary taxes would be to prevent inflation. Taxes are imposed either because the distribution of the burden of government expenditures brought about by inflation is not considered to be just or because of the fear of the allocational effects of inflation. If the latter were not feared, any distributional goals could be achieved by distributing to the "needy" as much "newly printed" money as was needed. The marginal social costs of both taxation and inflation are affected by both their distributional and allocational effects. But since taxes as the tools of a premeditated fiscal policy are usually more equitable than inflation, distributional effects would bring taxes to their capacity only if taxes were indeed more inflationary than deficit financing. But if the allocational effects of further taxation are socially more costly than those of marginal inflation, it is possible that, in spite of the usually lower social costs involved by the distributional effects of taxation, the marginal costs of taxation might exceed those of inflation. Allocational effects of taxation are thus what might bring it to its capacity.*

In the preceding section the different effects of taxation were discussed as if they had no interconnection. Actually, however, such interconnection is the core of the problem. If allocational effects of taxation could be disregarded, the rule of "minimum aggregate sacrifice" suggested by Edgeworth[10] would be the only and ideal rule to follow. Similarly, if distributional effects of taxation could be disregarded, the poll tax would be ideal, for, if the possibilities of suicide, emigration, and a deliberate decrease in birth rates are excluded, it has no allocational effects. In neither of these hypothetical cases would there be limits to taxation. Taxes might reach capacity just because distributional as well as announcement effects are socially important (and are reflected in social costs), so that neither Edgeworth's rule nor a poll tax are acceptable to society. It is because of distributional considerations that taxes with harmful allocational effects are used; and due to the bad allocational effects of some taxes, others which are less equitable are lived with. Thus, our statement that allocational effects of taxation are the ultimate causes for the possible existence of taxable capacity, though correct, concealed the interrelation between allocational effects and distributional considerations.

The main conclusion so far is that the limits of taxation depend on the allocational effects of taxation and of other sources of finance. When the allocational

* In Francis M. Bator's, *The Question of Government Spending* (New York, Harper & Brothers, 1960)—especially pp. 48-62—I have noticed several similarities to my own arguments.

effects are mentioned, one usually has in mind the effects of taxation on the supply and kinds of savings, on the size of aggregate investment, on the level of investment in risky enterprises, on the amount of work supplied and its intensity, on the methods of business finance, on the attitude towards wage increases, on the demand for liquid holdings, and on all other such effects of taxation which depend on tax formulae rather than merely upon the effects of taxes on real disposable incomes.

Some of the most serious distortional effects of taxes are probably in the field of output and input composition. Such effects usually result not from the level of taxation but from differences in the tax burden on various tax bases.[11] Clearly, it is impossible to discuss the comparative allocational effects of the various taxes without encompassing the whole field of public finance. In this context the only statement we venture to submit is that the wider the basis of taxes the less substitution effects they have and the higher their capacity. Taxes on economic surplus (rent) do not have, by definition, any allocational effects. If, for example, the definition of taxable income for income tax purpose included the money equivalents of "psychic income" from leisure, liquidity, safety, nonmonetary occupational advantages (or disadvantages), or from any other source, then an income tax certainly could not have the allocational effects—on the supplies of effort, risk-capital, occupational distribution, etc.—often associated with it. Income taxes might reach capacity because they are not that comprehensive, and therefore lower the relative prices of the sources of satisfaction not included in the tax basis. The higher are ordinary income taxes, the cheaper leisure and liquidity become and the more serious the allocational effects of the tax-caused changes in relative prices might become. To repeat, the more comprehensive the basis of a tax, the higher its capacity, because the higher is the element of surplus in the tax payments.

Needless to say, effective administration or, more exactly, an administration that is equally effective in covering all parts of the tax basis, is as important as a comprehensive basis.[12] The weaker the tax administration, the smaller the element of rent in the tax payments. For, say, in the case of an income tax, even if all economic activities are included in the tax basis, some will be administratively better covered than others; and even if the tax is universal, its effects will be close to those of a discriminating schedular tax. An important conclusion, therefore, is that an increase in the tax revenues of a government does not necessarily imply that the limits of taxation are closer. Since a new tax (or an improvement in the efficiency of the tax administration) might increase the element of rent in the tax system as a whole and thus significantly increase taxable capacity, that capacity is thus definitely not a constant amount or percentage.

The size of taxable capacity also depends, of course, on the allocational effects of inflationary deficit financing as well as on those of taxation, for it is determined by the comparison of the marginal social costs curve of a certain tax with the marginal social costs of deficit financing. And, to repeat, the whole argument of Functional Finance is a special case of the more general argument presented above: the marginal social costs of deficit financing during a depression are rather low. On the other hand, the allocational effects of inflation depend on the kind of inflation—open or repressed, on the degree of money illusion in the sense of a greater sensitivity to changes in money income than to changes in real income, on the relative strength of labor unions, on past experiences of inflation, on balance of payments problems, and so on. Since the marginal social costs of inflation may rise too, and rather quickly, it is more than possible that even though deficit financing should be used to finance a certain increase in government expenditures, it will reach its capacity rather soon, and more taxes should be used to finance any further increase in expenditure.

Interestingly, the size of national income and of national income *per capita* are not among the factors important in determining the size of taxable capacity. Obviously, *ceteris paribus,* the lower *per capita* income, the higher the disutility of a cut in disposable income, and therefore, unless the social benefits of government expenditure are much higher than in richer countries, the smaller the size of the capacity of government expenditures. But this has nothing to do with the size of taxable capacity as here defined.

To say that the size of income *per capita* is irrelevant to the problem of taxable capacity might contradict the familiar impression that poor and underdeveloped countries must have a lower taxable capacity. And, indeed, this might be true, but for other reasons. Taxable capacity might be relatively lower in underdeveloped countries if, say, because of poor tax administration, the "announcement effects" of taxation are stronger there, or if the social costs of inflation are lower. But the very poverty of underdeveloped countries is not relevant to the size of their taxable capacity; if they are too poor to afford more government expenditures, they may need foreign grants or loans, but inflationary deficit financing itself will not solve any purely economic problem. Given the size of government expenditures, it cannot involve lower real purchasing-power effects.

The relation between the distribution of income and the size of taxable capacity is less clear. It might be argued that the more equal this distribution, the higher the taxable capacity. For, as stated above, distributional considerations are responsible for the use of taxes with costly "announcement effects." In an economy with a completely equal distribution of income, a poll tax could not be logically opposed on distributional grounds, and it would be probably used as a single tax which hardly has a capacity. Yet this possible effect of an unequal distribution of income to decrease the size of taxable capacity is only an indirect one, since the determining factor here is the social attitude towards equality of income, an attitude which is not a single-value function of the existing distribution of income.

An important factor in the realities of the limits of taxation are the psychic costs of paying tax, costs which politicians will carefully heed because they are clearly relevant to the prospects of re-election. Economists should heed them too. Indeed, it is just as important to minimize the perceived costs as it is to minimize the material ones. It is well known that the "spite effects" of many taxes may be very serious, but perhaps even more serious may be the indirect emotional effects of paying taxes at all. To be sure, an aggrieved taxpayer will probably continue only for a short time "to hit back and inflict losses on the government"[13] by consciously reducing his work effort or his investment activities. But since taxpaying is not one single act, he may continue to feel hurt long afterwards, and that feeling in itself should be avoided if possible even when it does not result in direct economic losses.

Indeed much of the distinction between the various taxes, direct and indirect, and much of the political attractiveness of deficit financing, rests—as I shall argue—on differences in their psychic impact, with purely economic factors being only of secondary importance.

Needless to say, the structure of taxes in use affects their costs and thus their limit. But although classifications of taxes are abundant, the distinctions are not always very clear.

NOTES

1. The thesis is presented in Colin Clark's "Public Finance and Changes in the Value of Money," *The Economic Journal*, Vol. IV (December 1945), pp. 371-89; "The Danger Point in Taxes," *Harper's Magazine*, Vol. CC (December 1950), pp. 67-69. For some discussions on the subject, see Joseph A. Pechman and Thomas Mayer, "Mr. Colin Clark on the Limits of Taxation," *Review of Economics and Statistics*, Vol. XXXIV (August 1952), pp. 232-42. See also, Dan Throop Smith, "Note on Inflationary Consequences of High Taxation," *ibid.*, pp. 243-47; François Visine, "La Signification des Statistiques Fiscales et leur Utilisation," *Public Finance*, Vol. X, No. 1 (1955), pp. 7-81; P. D. Ojha, "Taxable Capacity in a Developing Economy," *The Indian Economic Journal*, Vol. II (January 1955), pp. 263-73. A comprehensive bibliography is given at the end of *The Limits of Taxable Capacity* (Princeton, N.J.: Tax Institute, Inc., 1953).

2. Abba P. Lerner, "Functional Finance and the Federal Debt," *Social Research* (February 1943), as reprinted in *Readings in Fiscal Policy* (London: George Allen & Unwin, 1955), pp. 468-78. The quotation is from p. 475. Italics supplied.

3. Cf. Simon Kuznets, "National Income and Taxable Capacity," *American Economic Review*, Vol. XXXII, No. 1, Supplement, Part 2 (March 1942), p. 42.

4. This definition is used explicitly by Monteath Douglas in "Taxable Capacity and British and Canadian Experience," *Limits of Taxable Capacity, op. cit.*, p. 31.

5. Cf. Kuznets, *op. cit.*, pp. 55-56.

6. William J. Fellner, "Postscript on War Inflation: A Lesson from World War II," reprinted in *Readings in Fiscal Policy, op. cit.*, pp. 137-54.

7. Cf. A. C. Pigou, *A Study in Public Finance*, 3rd ed. (London: Macmillan, 1947), p. 55.

8. *Ibid.*

9. Earl R. Rolph, *The Theory of Fiscal Economics* (Berkeley, Calif.: University of California Press, 1954), p. 14.

10. F. Y. Edgeworth, "The Pure Theory of Taxation," in *Papers Relating to Political Economy*, Vol. II (London: Macmillan, 1925), pp. 103-25.

11. For an empirical evaluation of the excise-tax effects of the corporation income, see Arnold C. Harberger, "The Corporation Income Tax: An Empirical Appraisal," in *Tax Revision Compendium*, Vol. 1 (Washington, D.C.: U. S. Government Printing Office, 1959), pp. 231-50.

12. That differences in the effectiveness of tax enforcement may have important results on the supply of labor was stressed by Richard Goode in "The Income Tax and the Supply of Labor," *Journal of Political Economy*, Vol. LVII, No. 5 (October 1949), reprinted in *Readings in the Economics of Taxation* (Homewood, Illinois: Irwin, 1959), pp. 456-69, and esp. pp. 466-67.

13. Richard A. Musgrave, *The Theory of Public Finance* (New York: McGraw-Hill, 1959), p. 240.

CHAPTER TWO

TAXES, MONEY, AND PRICES

Taxes may be classified in many ways, with the classifications serving different purposes. A common classification, into *progressive*, *proportional*, and *regressive* taxes, is that made according to their effects on the distribution of incomes. Some problems related to this classification will be discussed later.

Another classification is that of *partial* and *general* taxes. A truly general tax is one which is imposed at a constant marginal rate and applies equally to all relevant alternatives, thus having equal substitution ef-

fects. A partial tax is one which imposes a special tax
on specific ways of spending or earning money, or of
holding property. Actually, most taxes are somewhat
partial, discriminating sometimes openly against some
alternatives, as do excises and tariffs, and sometimes
disguisedly, as do income taxes which do not treat all
sources of income equally. But whereas partial taxes
necessarily change relative prices and outputs, general
taxes only reduce the purchasing-power for private
goods so that resources are released for government
expenditures. Government expenditures may themselves change relative prices if (as is usual) they are
not spent exactly on the resources released by the general taxes. But there is no "wedge" between prices for
producers and prices for consumers; there is just a
change in the structure of aggregate demand. Some
taxes like import or export are *necessarily* partial tariffs, but whether partiality is intrinsic or optional makes
little economic difference. The *extent* of the partiality,
on the other hand, may make a great difference, for,
generally, the wider the tax base the smaller are the
chances for tax-induced changes in the structure of
payments and/or expenditures. It should be made un-
equivocally clear that the intention to discriminate
hardly plays a role in this context. A tax on incomes
derived through corporations is, in an economy where
not all firms are corporations, a partial tax even if no
intention to discourage the corporate sector has ever
played any role in tax schemes.

Taxes may be imposed on incomes or on outlays,
they may be permanent or temporary, they may be imposed by the central government or some local body,
they may be collected at the source or assessed peri-
odically, they may be collected in cash or in kind, or
they may be general as far as the choices that any
single individual (or firm) may make, may discriminate between individuals or firms, may or may not

increase the price level, and, needless to say, classifications do not quickly come to an end.

We have not mentioned the famous classification of taxes into direct and indirect taxes for the simple reason that the meaning of that classification is not easily agreed upon. According to the United Nations definition,[1] direct taxes on households and private nonprofit institutions includes all taxes levied or charged on their incomes, while taxes on goods and services that are chargeable to business expenses and taxes on the possession or use of goods and services by households are treated as indirect taxes. The main categories of indirect taxes, according to the U.N. definition, are, import, export and excise duties, local rates, entertainment duties, betting taxes, sales taxes, business licenses, stamp duties, motor vehicle duties, and taxes on the operation of wireless and television sets, etc., including real estate and land taxes when not considered merely administrative devices for the collection of income taxes. The common denominator of this definition is the existence of a market price which is different from the factor-costs of production. Sometimes it is implied, or even stated explicitly, that the basic difference between direct and indirect taxes is that the latter increase the price level.

Bent Hansen, in his *Economic Theory of Fiscal Policy*, makes this claim very clearly.

> The distinction between so-called direct and indirect taxes is arbitrary in several respects. Sometimes the tax-subject is the decisive factor. If the buyer consumer is himself responsible for the tax payment, the tax is not always included in the price level. . . . For example, compare a general turnover tax which is imposed at a rate of 5% on consumer goods and a general consumption tax which is imposed at a rate of 5% on declared income minus saving. If we ignore evasion and the point

of time when the payment takes place, there is no difference between these two taxes. Despite this, the former will, other things being equal, raise the price level (at market prices) by 5% while the latter will leave the price level unchanged.[2]

Basically, this statement is the foundation for many of Hansen's suggestions for stable-price policies which are based on offsetting increases in wages or other components of costs by decreasing indirect taxes, which are also components of costs, and by letting increased income taxes take care of the inflationary gap that would have otherwise occurred. The idea is that increases in cost elements could be offset by decreases in other cost elements, achieved by cuts in existing indirect taxes or increases in direct subsidies. Under special conditions and where the stability of some price index is of great importance, it could even be a wise policy, if indeed indirect taxes do raise prices while direct taxes do not.

Yet in spite of the obvious importance of this assumption for his analysis and conclusions, Hansen does not attempt to justify it. It seems to him obvious and, indeed, it is usually granted as such. It is of interest that while the distinction between direct and indirect taxes is often admitted to be arbitrary, the inflationary impact of indirect taxation is a common worry. But why attribute such impact to indirect taxes only? Why should a tax paid directly by households always be less inflationary than that paid directly by firms? Whatever one's views of the Quantity Theory as a predictive model, any price change must necessarily depend on changes in M, V, or T. If changes in M and/or T are ruled out, V—that is, the transactions velocity of money—has to carry all the burden. This is not too much of a burden if V does not really depend on any factor, and is completely arbitrary. But if V were that free, the Quantity Theory would obviously be devoid of all content; moreover, such freedom also implies that the price level is completely arbitrary, and therefore it would be silly to attempt to stabilize it, as Bent Hansen does.

But if the velocity of circulation *is* a function of some factors, and if indirect taxes, as compared to direct taxes, really do increase V, as the standard conclusions require, those factors must necessarily be affected differently by the two kinds of taxes. Such factors might be the frequency and regularity of receipts and disbursements in the community and the correspondence of timing between receipts and disbursements, expectations of the community as to future incomes and prices (including the rate of interest), the ease of lending and/or borrowing and the stage of development of the credit system and the extent to which the community uses it, the rapidity of the transportation of money, saving, and hoarding propensities,[3] and . . . the list might be long but I should not like to end it with "and what not."

WHY INDIRECT TAXES RAISE THE PRICE LEVEL

Although it is usually granted that a substitution of indirect taxes for direct taxes could change V by changing the structure of payments, the nature and direction of the change are themselves uncertain. They depend on such institutional details as whether indirect taxes are imposed at the retail, wholesale, or manufacturing level; on whether income taxes are deducted at the source; and on other factors that might affect the timing of tax collections. We shall return to this problem later; for the time being, let us assume that no difference obtains between direct and indirect taxes, as far as their effect on V is concerned.[4]

If so, what are the grounds for the common assumption that indirect taxes are the more inflationary?

The assumption might be due simply to an illegitimate extension of the results of partial-equilibrium analysis of the effects of partial taxes. Certainly, partial taxes, by affecting relative supplies of goods and services, may increase some prices absolutely as well as relatively. In partial-equilibrium analysis it is considered legitimate to neglect the effects (supposedly negligible) of a tax on a given commodity on the prices of all other goods. Each tax on a single commodity seems therefore to increase one price. And it follows, speciously, that many such taxes necessarily do increase the price level. Needless to say, the rise in the price of the taxed goods under a partial tax is caused by the cut in its production (and, presumably, the rise in the production of all other commodities and services combined). To have the same effect with a general tax, unemployment must occur.

It might be argued that in a capital-formation model even a general sales tax that exempts savings is a partial tax, and that therefore, even with money supply and velocity constant, the price level will rise if measured by an index of only those goods and services which are not tax exempt. But this argument simply will not stand up in the comparison of a turnover tax with an expenditure tax, since both exempt savings. And, obviously, it would have no relevance whatsoever in an all-consumption model. Also, it is not true that indirect taxes do necessarily exempt savings (although they do exempt hoardings as long as unspent). Taxes on consumer durables, on equipment, and on materials for buildings are common in many countries. Yet even if in a capital-formation model the indirect taxes are true consumption taxes and therefore only partial (to some extent), the rise in consumption prices attributed to indirect taxes must necessarily depend on a cut in total real consumption and, assuming no unemployment, an increase in real capital formation. If this does take place, there might be a negative inflationary impact in the long run.

One may argue that our difficulties are caused by rigid "Quantity Theory" reasoning. Income taxes do not raise prices because they reduce disposable incomes. Naturally a substitution of a sales tax for an income tax should raise prices, for the abolishment (or decrease) in income tax increases disposable income and thus increases the demand for—and ultimately the prices of—goods and services. As a matter of fact, the need for a rise in prices seems only too clear. Consumption depends on real disposable income, and if after the decrease in income tax and the increase in indirect taxes, prices would not have risen, then real disposable incomes would, and with them also consumption expenditures. Prices, therefore, have to rise.

But let us be more careful. First, to make things easier for ourselves, let us use Patinkin's model[5] where consumption is a function of real disposable income, the rate of interest, and real money balances. Let us also assume an all-consumption model, that labor is the only factor of production (that is, the wage bill is equal to national income), that government expenditures are constant in real terms, and that the nominal amount of money is fixed. Suppose that as a result of the increase in disposable money income which follows the substitution of, say, proportional, indirect taxes for income taxes, there is a general rise in the price level equal to the rate of the indirect taxes. This rise in prices together with the cut in the income tax would leave real disposable income at the same level, but decrease real money balances. This decline in real money balances, however, would necessarily exert deflationary pressures in the market for commodities, with the result that the price level would begin to fall. But a fall in the price level including indirect taxes would mean a price level excluding taxes lower than that prevailing under the income tax. Real wages having risen for the employers, they would presumably hire less labor services, and unemployment would develop, forcing down the money wage bill, which equals disposable money income. The cut in money disposable income would reduce demand still further, and the process would continue until the price level, including taxes, and disposable money income returned to their income-tax levels.

I am aware that empirical investigations have not established a strong real balance effect in the consumption and investment functions in all countries, in all periods, but surely this cannot detract from the importance of such effects as equilibrating factors. The real balance effect of the temporary price rise will also—as part of the adjustment process—raise the interest rate, by increasing the demand for money balances, or, in a Keynesian model, by increasing the demand for money for transaction purposes, which will result in a fall in the price of bonds.* In any case the rise in the rate of interest might strengthen the deflationary consequences of the real balance effects in the market for goods and services.

We have thus reached the perhaps obvious conclusion that in an all-consumption model, with labor being the only factor of production, there is no difference between a tax on all incomes and a tax on all expenditures. Since once reached it seems almost too clear, I believe that these results would hold even with more "realistic assumptions," as long as both direct

---

* Also, as long as market prices have not returned to their income-tax level, there will be an increase in T, the total of monetary transactions to be made with the given supply of money, since the sum of money transactions connected with tax payments is increased. This should be an additional factor working towards reducing the price level.

and indirect taxes were general. To be sure, the model used assumed no price rigidity, and in that sense it may be ill-equipped to describe conditions in most modern economics. But if we assume that prices (or wages) cannot go down, unemployment will occur, unless money supply be expanded to offset the real balance effect of the nonequilibrium rise in the market prices. Once this is assumed, we might as well go back to Quantity Theory.

Many economists have felt uneasy about this apparent contradiction between the conclusions of an analysis in terms of aggregate demand and the direct conclusions of the Quantity-Theory assumptions. Richard Goode, discussing a situation in which a government substitutes a retail sales tax for an individual income tax at a time when there is neither inflationary nor deflationary pressure, notes: "In order for market prices of taxed commodities to rise by the full amount of the tax and all other prices to remain unchanged, consumers or some other sector must increase spending by the full amount of the sales tax revenue."[6] In other words, Goode recognized that MV must rise, which means, if M is constant, that V must rise. But why should V rise? G. F. Break, who, following Rolph and H. G. Brown, claims that the consumption taxes will not be shifted forward in higher prices but will instead be shifted backward in lower money returns to factors of production, bases his demonstration on the assumption that money consumption is related to past disposable income, and that therefore consumption demand remains stable in the face of the change from an income tax to a sales tax.[7] This device, however, only postpones the problem to another period, and the proof, in any event, is only of a specific case. John Due says reproachfully of J. S. Mill's conclusion—that a general sales tax could not be shifted forward in higher prices—that his "reasoning is based on

a rigid application of the quantity theory of money."[8]
His own explanations (*ibid.*, p. 261)—that an increase
in government expenditures and in indirect taxes will
raise aggregate money demand because of the balanced-budget multiplier—is inapplicable when a differential analytical approach is used, that is, when
government expenditures are assumed to be constant
and only the methods of finance are changed.

THE LOCATION OF TAXES AND THE PRICE LEVEL

We have overstated our case intentionally. Although, as already stated, the effect of a switch from
income taxes to indirect taxes on the frequency and
regularity of receipts and disbursements in the community and the correspondence of timing between
them could go both ways, there are indeed reasons to
assume that it will raise V nevertheless. Some increase
in V may be caused by expectations of further rise
in price created by the original rise. More important
might be the change in the ease of borrowing and the
stage of development of the credit system and the
extent to which the community uses it. It is a fact that
the degree of development of the credit system in an
economy is much higher for firms than for households. Thus while most young persons have before
them a long life of productive work, they usually cannot easily borrow against it.* To get a loan, one usually
has to own a marketable asset. And it so happens
that firms, not households, own most marketable assets. For a household as such it is very difficult indeed to borrow in order to pay for consuming either
private nondurables or public goods. Firms on the
other hand have access to the credit outlets and know
that they may rely on them in cases of emergency.

* The development of installment-plan purchases doubtlessly
somewhat changes this.

Thus, the demand of business for cash balances would be comparatively small (in relation to transactions) in comparison to households' demand even if all other conditions were equal in respect to both.

Yet other conditions are not equal. The costs of holding money are often higher for business than for households either because of differences in opportunity, or because, according to Hicks,[9] a business firm that typically has larger amounts of cash to invest gets higher returns since net expected interest increases with the quantity of money. It has also been recently demonstrated that business receipts and expenditures are more closely meshed than are personal receipts and expenditures.[10] There might be conditions of economies of scale in the use of money,[11] and if so, since business firms encounter larger volumes of transactions than do most individuals, they will surely hold less money per unit of transactions than do individuals. For all these reasons there is a very considerable difference between the velocity of circulation of money held by business and that held by households. As a matter of fact, business velocity of bank deposits has been estimated to be from ten to thirteen times the household velocity,[12] while the turnover of business holdings of money and demand deposits has been estimated to be from two to three times the turnover of households' holdings.[13]

Since there are such great differences between the V_b—velocity of circulation of business money—and V_h—the velocity of circulation of household money—a switch from direct to indirect taxes may, indeed, raise the price level by the very fact that in the case of indirect taxation, the "tax collectors," that is the firm, have a very high V.* M must rise only to the

---

* Still, since the rise in the price level raises T, as argued in note on p. 31, the rise in PT will be proportional to the rise in V, and the rise in P, the price level itself, will be lower than the relative increase in the velocity of transactions.

extent that the rise in V, due to the change in the structure of taxes, is not sufficient to allow the necessary rise in the price level without unemployment. Indeed, the rise in M might occur automatically. If, for example, the income tax used to be withheld at the beginning of each "week," but the indirect taxes are paid during the week at a constant rate, then, *ceteris paribus*, after the former is replaced by the latter, there must be a fall in government money balances—that is, an increase in M. But that is only a possibility. More important, perhaps, is increased bank borrowing by firms. As stated, firms are close to the channels of credits, yet even they usually do not get all the bank loans they want because of some credit rationing. They may hit upon the opportunity of the imposition of (or increase in) indirect taxes to get more bank loans.

Even so, there is no guarantee that MV would indeed increase sufficiently for prices to rise in correspondence to the rate of indirect taxes. In this case, there would either be some fall in prices—excluding taxes—or unemployment; or in order to fight unemployment, there would be a rise in money supply originated intentionally by the government itself.

The inflationary impact usually ascribed to indirect taxes should therefore be attributed to monetary conditions. If direct taxes were accompanied by increases in MV, they would have very similar effects.

SHIFTING AND ATTEMPTED SHIFTING

In the case of most partial outlay taxes the intention of the government is that the formal taxpayer, the firm, will be able to shift the taxes to buyers of the taxed products, a shift which can be easily facilitated by raising the price level. But raising the price level does not guarantee that the taxes are truly shifted, for the increased cost of living may bring about increased wages, and so on. As Musgrave has made only too clear,[14] shifting must involve a change in relative prices, and whether such a change really does take place needs examination. In any event, a distinction must be made between shifting taxes and attempts at shifting. Such attempts might be inflationary if the government, obliged to keep full employment, increases the quantity of money whenever there is a danger that some price or wage policies might cause unemployment.

In such a case, monetary "policy" has to accommodate itself to changes in wages: If the price of labor is overincreased and unemployment develops, the monetary authorities must increase the money supply so that rising commodity-prices will lower real wages to the equilibrium level.[15] The terms *labor standard* or *wage standard* have been proposed for such cases where, instead of having monetary standards determine the general level of money wages, the level of money wages determines the quantity of money, the price level, and ultimately, the foreign exchange value of the currency.

It is self-evident that such policies yield an extremely strong power to labor unions—a power which, like any power, can and may be misused. But not so easily recognized is the fact that in a democratic society, the very same policies yield an equally strong power to employers and their organizations. Indeed, the latter are put into an excellent bargaining—sometimes almost a blackmail—position versus the government and the monetary authorities. Since the cooperation of employers is essential if the declared policy of no unemployment is to be carried through, employers can always raise prices without worrying about demand elasticities. The powers of the unions and of the employers are in this case far from being "countervailing." But here too, and in a much more direct fashion, one force begets another by its very existence.[16]

If the assumption that money supply is an exogenous variable has to be removed from an analysis, it is
obvious that discussions of tax incidence should also
take into consideration the possible effects of taxation
on money supply. Where labor unions are powerful
and spoiled, as they may very well be if the country
is under an absolute wage standard, they might ask
for higher gross wages for their members whenever
any increase in taxation, direct or indirect, hits workers, and especially whenever such an increase seems
to labor leaders to disturb the distributional relationships last agreed upon. As a matter of fact, this is
exactly what they do in situations of this sort, and in
the case of indirect taxes there is usually an automatic mechanism for compensating wage earners for
the indirect taxes paid by them (that is, of course,
linking wages to a cost-of-living index that includes
indirect taxes). Wages have been, at least partly,
automatically escalated to cost-of-living or similar
indices in Chile, Denmark, Finland, France, Israel,
Italy, and Norway. Sliding-scale agreements are limited to some branches of industry in England and to
a rather small fraction of the working class in the
United States. The cost of living, however, is naturally
an important factor in wage negotiations wherever
such negotiations take place.[17]

Although demands for inclusion of direct taxes
into the cost-of-living index so that wage earners will
be automatically compensated for any increase in
income taxes too, have not yet been accepted, it is
often clear that any increase in the income tax that
affects the price-index family budgets is compensated
by increases in wages the next time they are adjusted.* General increases in nominal wages will not

* In Sweden, the trade union movement even attempts to
forecast the effects of its wage claims on prices and to write
up the claim in accordance with a multiplier formula which

be strongly opposed by employers under the circumstances, for they "shift" them forward in higher prices the way they "shift" upwards in higher prices any burden imposed upon them. The employers do not worry about being unsuccessful because the full employment policy of the government (if extreme) guarantees them effectively against failure. Any equilibrium level of prices and money wages is thus unstable, and a potential price-wage spiral merely waits for a push that will start it. Income taxes, like all taxes, might be among the many possible reasons that might start such a cumulative up-movement of prices and wages, especially if they are not imposed in a way that both labor unions and employers accept as fair. Each group will struggle to redistribute the national output in its favor by raising wages or prices, and neither has much to lose from a new round of the spiral.

The case just described is possibly extreme, but in less extreme cases there might also be persistent *attempts* to shift the burdens of a general tax through a change in the absolute price level in the hope that, ultimately, relative prices will also change and the taxes will thus be at least partly shifted. Obviously, if the government is unwilling to resist fully the tendencies towards monetary expansion that can result through higher taxation, tax increases might be responsible for a more or less commensurate income increase.

Our argument raises the possibility that a major part of the discussions concerning the incidence of income taxes has been based not on disagreement on facts but rather on a lack of true communication between the disputants, whom we shall call for brevity's

---

takes into account also the marginal rate of taxation. See Sir Dennis H. Robertson, "Creeping Inflation," in *Economic Commentaries* (London: Staples Press, 1956), p. 124, fn.

sake "businessmen" and "academic economists." To-day, as in the days of the British Colwyn Committee, most "businessmen" are confident that income taxes on profits are, at least to some extent, passed on to buyers in the form of higher prices. The "academic economists," on the other hand, have yielded some ground. They now recognize that their basic attitude rests on the assumption that the income tax is a truly general tax which is imposed on *all alternative* sources of real income, and do not hesitate to admit therefore that a partial (and discriminating) tax could be at least partly shifted.

Clearly, all practical cases are partial. No general tax is imposed in practice on real income which also includes the utilities of leisure, liquidity, safety, and the nonmonetary advantages (and disadvantages) of certain occupations. And because of either the progression in rates which makes loss-offsets useless for this purpose for cases where the economic loss still leaves taxable income, or because of a lack of full loss-offsets, income taxes rarely take into full consideration the *differences* in the uncertainty that is involved in the various alternative enterprises. In addition, since all income taxes are imposed in a given geographical and political area, taxpayers can avoid taxation by simply moving into another area. Also, from the administrative point of view the objective possibilities of the tax assessor to assess income correctly vary considerably from one industry to another. Lastly, in the case of an oligopolistic market structure, "economists" do not usually insist too strongly on their basic point—that income taxes are not shifted. It is easy to devise models of oligopolistic behavior where taxes are "shifted" because they provide an opportunity to overcome some obstacles to joint maximization of profits. The essence of this alleged behavior is that there is some self-imposed moral restraint on net profits rather than on gross profits. It is difficult to evaluate this last argument when it is applied not to a small number of firms but to a sector with great importance in the economy, where changes in the prices charged by that sector must bring about changes in other prices as well. Also it is not clear what determines the magnitude of the "just" net rate of return and what it includes as part of the rate of return. In any case this ends the list of the major concessions made by "academic economists" to "businessmen."

Basically, these concessions are based on the argument that, as actually partial taxes, both "general" income and outlay taxes have substitution effects reflected in changes in the relative supplies of goods and services, so that, like all partial taxes, they may be partly shifted. But a truly general tax could not— by definition—be shifted, for the simple reason that *when everybody shifts a tax, it must be shifted to nobody.* The exceptions granted, the general rule which still seems obvious to most "economists" is: as long as marginal rates of taxes are lower than one hundred per cent, any output that yields maximum profits before an imposition of an increase of an income tax, also yields the maximum (though, of course, less) *net* profits. Since relative outputs are unchanged by the income tax, so are relative prices. That is, there is no tax shifting, for tax shifting must take the form of changes in the *relative* prices of goods and services including, naturally, the prices of all factors of production.

The arguments of the "economists" convince (as they should) most economists, but few "businessmen." Yet the attitudes of "businessmen" and "economists" are not necessarily incompatible. Obviously, relative prices either change or do not change, but relative prices may keep unchanged while absolute prices (that is, the absolute price level) do change. We suggest that misunderstanding occurs because at least some "businessmen" do not have relative prices in mind at all. It is probable that their argument is plainly that income taxes increase the absolute price level of products; that is, businessmen attempt, in any market structure where they determine product prices at all, to shift these taxes forward. Whether such attempts are successful or not depends on what happens to relative prices, that is, on whether the prices of the factors of production that businessmen employ rise to the same extent. But an unsuccessful attempt implies that the income taxes have not been shifted, not that prices have not been raised. If that is really what "businessmen" have argued, they must have been perplexed when their experience has been confronted by arguments about marginal costs, marginal firms, and a maximum which remains the maximum.

Strangely enough, although the whole argument refers to a general (as distinct from partial) income tax, so that *forward* shifting of a general income tax necessarily *implies a higher price level*, only a few economists have challenged the businessmen's views on incidence by the counterargument that with a given supply of money and a given velocity of circulation the price level of a given output is given too. This is quite unfortunate, for the assumption of a given money supply, if unshared by the businessmen's representatives, might have been at the bottom of a perhaps specious argument between those who claim that general income taxes cannot possibly be shifted and those who insist that they raise prices. Businessmen's opinion that income taxes are in effect "concealed sales taxes" should not have puzzled economists, for income taxes *are* concealed sales taxes and sales taxes *are* concealed income taxes to the extent that both are truly general taxes; both are taxes on real incomes. As we have already stressed, there is obviously a difference between the incidence of a general income tax and of partial taxes like excise or custom duties, but the sources of this difference lie in the partiality of the latter taxes.

Our belief that businessmen have meant "inflationary impact" when they have discussed the shifting of income taxes gets some support from the thought that from an egotistical point of view businessmen have reasons to support the no-shifting argument. Also it is often noted that the opinion expressed by businessmen that income taxes are shifted to consumers in higher prices cannot be easily reconciled with its accompanying belief that the tax has had undesirable effects on business performance and investment. This inconsistency is of special relevance to the issue of the "double taxation" of corporations which exists where a corporation profits tax like the U.S. Corporation Income Tax—a partial income tax—is imposed on corporations in addition to the income tax on dividends that shareholders pay. Obviously, if corporation taxes were indeed fully shifted there would be no double taxation at all, and corporations would serve only as tax collectors for the government, just as they collect for the Treasury the income tax deducted at the source from their employees. This becomes a *non sequitur*, however, if all that businessmen mean when claiming that both general income tax and partial profits taxes are shifted in higher prices for consumers is simply that they raise absolute prices, which does not necessarily imply that they change relative prices and therefore does not imply that they shift the taxes. In which case, there is no more any logical inconsistency between the complaint of businessmen that income taxes curtail the real funds available for investments and their arguments that they are successful in "shifting" income taxes.

Virtually the only way to find out what either "businessmen" or "academic economists" do have in mind is to ask them—which is easier said than done. "Academic economists" have often illustrated a special gift for misunderstanding simple common-sense questions. For example, there has been a series of recurring attacks by important public finance economists on the assumption of forward shifting of outlay taxes. These economists claim that outlay taxes do not increase the price level—which may well be true—and mistakenly conclude that therefore they are shifted backward in reduced factor payments. But as Musgrave has shown, the real issue should not be what happens to the price level. Whether the general price level rises as a result of a substitution of outlay taxes for an equi-revenue income tax, or whether it is unchanged while prices excluding the outlay taxes fall, depends on monetary assumptions. Changes in the supply of money have an incidence of their own, but changes in the absolute price level have very little to do with the incidence of taxation, which is a function of relative price changes. If neither the relative prices of the factors of production nor those of goods and services are changed by a tax, then this tax is not shifted at all. In effect, it is meaningless to argue that such a tax is borne by consumers and not by producers, or vice versa—for they are the same persons! "Businessmen" know, of course, whether they do or do not raise prices. Indeed, there are often well-recorded price statistics which give a rather clear answer to such questions. But with an elastic money supply there would always be the problem of the arbitrariness of any specific date for incidence calculations.

NOTES

1. See, for example, *A System of National Accounts and Supporting Tables*, Studies in Methods, Series F, No. 2 (United Nations, 1960), p. 36.

2. See Bent Hansen, *The Economic Theory of Fiscal Policy* (London: Allen & Unwin, 1958), p. 220.

3. In listing the factors affecting V, I have been greatly assisted by Lester Chandler, *The Economics of Money and Banking* (New York: Harper, 1948), p. 546.

4. Cf. Richard A. Musgrave, *The Theory of Public Finance* (New York: McGraw-Hill, 1959), pp. 364-70.

5. Fully presented in Don Patinkin's *Money, Interest and Prices* (Evanston, Illinois: Row, Peterson, 1956).

6. See R. Goode, "Discussion," *American Economic Review*, Vol. XLIII (May 1953), p. 541.

7. G. F. Break, "Excise Tax Burdens and Benefits," *American Economic Review*, Vol. XLIV (September 1954), p. 581.

8. John F. Due, "Toward a General Theory of Sales Incidence," *Quarterly Journal of Economics*, Vol. LXVII (May 1953), p. 259 fn.

9. J. R. Hicks, "A Suggestion for Simplifying the Theory of Money," *Readings in Monetary Theory* (New York: Blakiston, 1951), p. 19.

10. See John J. McCall, "Differences between the Personal Demand for Money and the Business Demand for Money," *The Journal of Political Economy*, Vol. LXVIII (August 1960), pp. 358-68.

11. W. J. Baumol, "The Transactions Demand for Cash: An Inventory Theoretic Approach," *Quarterly Journal of Economics*, Vol. LXVI (November 1952), pp. 545-56.

12. The separate mimeographed estimates were made by Mary Petty, Gary S. Becker, and John J. McCall. See footnote 10 in McCall's article, *op. cit.*

13. This estimate made by Mrs. Petty.

14. See, especially, Chapter 15 and 16 of his *The Theory of Public Finance, op. cit.*

15. See J. R. Hicks, "Economic Foundations of Wage Policy," *The Economic Journal,* Vol. LXV (September 1956); and A. P. Lerner, "Monetary Policy under the Wage Standard" (Jerusalem, Israel, mimeographed). An excellent exposition of the conditions underlying a wage standard is to be found in Gosta Rehn, "The Problems of Stability: An Analysis and Some Policy Proposals," in *Wages Policy under Full Employment,* ed. and trans. by Ralph Turvey (London: William Hodge, 1952), pp. 39-49.

16. Cf. M. Bronfenbrenner, "Some Neglected Implications of Secular Inflation," *Post Keynesian Economics,* ed. by Kenneth K. Kurihara (New Brunswick, N.J.: Rutgers University Press, 1954), p. 36; and Henri Aujac, "Inflation as the Monetary Consequence of the Behaviour of Social Groups," *International Economic Papers,* No. 4 (1954), pp. 109-23.

17. Cf. C. Bresciani-Turroni, "Working of the Sliding Scale Applied to Wages in Italy," Banco di Roma, *Review of the Economic Conditions in Italy,* Vol. X (November 1956), pp. 519-47; and also Jørgen Pedersen, "Wage-Fixing According to the Price Index," *International Economic Papers,* No. 4 (1954), pp. 70-108, esp. pp. 85-92; Amotz Morag, "Escalator Clauses and Indirect Taxes," *The Indian Economic Journal,* Vol. III (October 1955), pp. 154-67.

CHAPTER THREE

THE DEFLATIONARY
EFFECTS OF TAXES

Functional Finance tells us that the purpose of taxation should be to cut down private spending, when necessary, to prevent excessive aggregate demand and inflation.[1] An implication of this principle is that, since their effects on aggregate demand might differ, two equi-revenue taxes are not necessarily perfect substitutes as anti-inflationary fiscal tools: "The more they are paid at the expense of potential savings, the higher the taxes have to be to secure a given restraint on spending."[2] Following Kaldor, one may call the net expenditure-restraining effects of taxation per unit of receipt its "economic efficiency."[3]

Possible reasons for unequal "economic efficiency" of the various equi-revenue taxes—and there is an infinite number of taxes if any formula is taken as a separate tax—are: (a) differences in the distributional impact of the taxes; (b) allocational effects due to differences in tax formulae; (c) "money illusions" of various kinds; and (d) the nature of the tax base. A tax on irregular incomes—like those on occasional capital gains, estate taxes, and excess-profits taxes based on a standard of true normal profits—is less "efficient" than a tax on ordinary incomes. Similarly if the tax itself rather than its base is irregular, it will have a relatively low "economic efficiency" since the reduction in the normal disposable income may be relatively slight.

Obviously, for purposes of *fiscal policy* it is important to know what the "economic efficiency" of each tax is, so that what money yield of any tax is economically equivalent—*that is, cuts aggregate demand to the same extent and has identical effects on the equilibrium price level*—to that of any other tax can be easily determined. All discussions of the inflationary significance of a government budget, balanced or unbalanced, must pay attention to possible differences in the "economic efficiency" of the various taxes. To repeat Carl Shoup's words:

. . . when the discussion centers on degrees of employment, and on inflation or deflation, equality of revenue-raising power is no longer an appropriate unit for comparison. A more relevant unit would be the extent to which the tax forces a reduction in consumer spending or in investment spending; that is, the extent to which the tax forces the private sector of the economy to release economic resources that the government may then hire.[4]

But does the comparative "economic efficiency" of taxes have other implications? Is it one of the criteria that should be taken into account when choosing between taxes? Specifically, if two taxes are similar in all other respects,* but tax A requires, because of its lower "economic efficiency," more money yield than tax B, should tax A be preferred to tax B, or not?

Since Kaldor lists the relative "inefficiency" of income taxes as an argument for an expenditure tax, he apparently believes that the comparative "economic efficiency" of a tax must be taken into account when choosing from alternative taxes. To George F. Break, on the other hand, the efficiency argument seems "a considerable overestimation of the advantages of economizing on tax revenues, which are not a scarce resource."[5] I intend to rediscuss this problem here.

The very question would undoubtedly be hard to explain not only to a Secretary of the Treasury, but also to any layman who naturally would tend to think of it in terms of the comparative burdens imposed by unequal money taxes on a single individual. For the layman the superiority of the smaller money tax is only too obvious. Since prices are given to him, a lower money tax *is* a lower real tax, as far as he is concerned; even if the two unequal money taxes reduce his current resource-using expenditures to the same extent, the lower money tax leaves him with more money balance and/or bonds, so that he *must* be better off. This, incidentally, is why saving and,

---

* Shoup (*ibid.*, p. 267) notes that "there is no *a priori* rule in this matter to be applied in advance; we cannot say that, among taxes having the same resource releasing power, we shall always want to select the one that yields the largest revenue." That is true, of course; but the same might be said of any criterion for tax policy.

even compulsory saving, is considered preferable by *any single individual* to paying the very same amount of money in taxes. (By savings we shall henceforth mean nonresources-using savings, that is, savings which are not investment in the national accounting sense.) Indeed this is the basis for various tax schemes that have been often proposed, and sometimes also implemented, the essence of which is to induce individuals to save more and to pay less in income taxes and other taxes as well.[6] Savings are politically less painful than taxation, not only because they involve no compulsion (unless the savings are compulsory) but also because, unlike the taxpayer, the saver is compensated for the cut in his present consumption by bonds and/or money balances.

IS THE ECONOMIC EFFICIENCY OF TAXES IMPORTANT?

From the above argument, it follows that if an individual has to cut to a *given level* the present use of some *specific* resources that are needed for the government's program, he will prefer that this be done by "excises," that is, by partial taxes which discriminate against these resources or the commodities produced from them rather than by supposedly nondiscriminating taxes. Discriminating taxes, having substitution effects in addition to their income effects, will require less money revenue to achieve their purpose in this case. Thus the argument that excises impose an excess burden in comparison to an equivalent income tax[7] is, *for the case of a single individual*, completely reversed when the function of the alternative taxes is to release a given amount of specific real resources, and when the excise discriminates against those specific resources. (Although the argument was put in terms of *direct vs. indirect taxes*, its essence is a comparison of the welfare effects of *partial vs. general taxes.*) This is illustrated graphically in Figure 4.

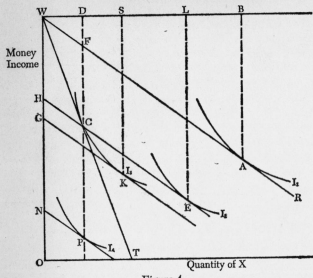

Figure 4

In Figure 4, *WR* is the pre-tax price line for a commodity *X*, *WB* the amount of *X* bought at this price by an individual, and *AB* the amount of money income spent by him on *X*. An imposition of an excise on *X* changes the price line from *WR* to *WT*; the amount of *X* bought falls to *WD* and the new amount of money income spent on *X* is *CD*. But out of *CD*, *CF* represents the payment of the excise on *X*. If the government is indifferent to sources of revenues (as long as they are tax revenues) and is interested only in their money size, an income tax *HW* may be substituted for the excise tax *CF*. Since *HW* is equal to *CF*, the government still gets the same amount of tax revenue from the individual. But this substitution, to which the government is completely indifferent, is in favor of the individual who is transferred by it from indifference curve I_3 to the higher indifference curve I_2. Indeed, the burden of paying CF as an excise tax is equal to the burden of paying WG as income tax, as both leave the individual on the same indifference curve, I_3. HG represents, so the argument ends, the excess burden of the excise.

Yet, although the individual is better off if he pays HW in income tax rather than paying the same money amount, CF, as an excise, his consumption of X under the income tax is WL, while it is only WD under the excise tax on X. That E must be to the right of C is the core of the excess-burden-of-indirect-taxes argument. If an income tax were also to cut the individual's consumption of X to WD, the revenue from it would have to be increased to WN, and the individual transferred to position P, which is on indifference curve I_4, the lowest of the four. If the government is interested in releasing BD of X from consumption, it should be indifferent as to whether it gets WN as income-tax revenue, or only WH as excise-tax revenues. But, in this case, the individual would definitely prefer the excise. HN is, so to speak, the excess burden of general income taxes.

It should be stressed that the argument does not depend on an assumption that the government will not bid up the prices of the resources it needs. Even if the price of X is bid up, an excise on X that yields a given revenue will release more X for the government than will an income tax yielding the same revenue; hence as X prices are bid up by the government, more money will still be needed by the government to buy a given amount of resources.

No changes are introduced into the argument if the discriminating feature of the taxes is not directed towards the use of some *specific* resources but against current consumption in general. If Figure 4 is to represent this case, too, its horizontal axis should signify current consumption, and the vertical axis, changes (additions to or substractions from) in money assets and bonds, that is, savings or dissavings in a given period. In short, the argument—if the government is interested in reducing the consumption of the individual to a given level—is unchanged.

Note that this argument, like that of Miss Joseph, applies only to the case of one individual and is valid only when the pre-tax allocation of resources has been optimal. Moreover, the whole argument disregards completely the existence in the economy of a transformation curve between commodities. The excise burden argument is now out of favor mainly due to the methodological criticism of Milton Friedman and the substantial criticism of I. M. D. Little, Earl R. Rolph, and George F. Break.[8] The reversal of the argument here should be taken as an additional criticism of it, rather than as a new "theorem."

The case of one individual, however, is not very interesting. Indeed, if he constitutes a very small part of the total community, it might be legitimately argued that the effect of his adjustment on total output might be disregarded; and if so, it should also be a matter of irrelevance to the government just how much will be released by him. The major problem, therefore, is whether it is valid to generalize from this analysis to the community at large. Clearly, excises on goods and/or services which are needed by the government for its own expenditures are more "efficient" than general taxes, for, if variable costs are assumed, they reduce the money costs of the government purchases.[9] The question, however, is whether that result is important.

At first, the answer to that question would seem to be an unqualified "No!" It has become rather common to state that taxes as such do not constitute an independent burden on private groups, and that one "must look to government expenditures for evidence concerning costs in the sense of what private groups are forced to give up as takers because the government acquires the use of resources."[10] In other words, the gross burden of taxation—which does not take into account the benefits from the government expenditures—is determined only by the size of the government expenditures. This, of course, neglects some important factors, for the aggregate burden of taxation also depends upon: (a) its distribution among the various income groups; (b) tax effects on the supply of resources both in the short and the long run; (c) the resources employed by both the government and the taxpayers in connection with the collection of taxes. But the comparative "economic efficiency" of the various taxes, and this is the main point of the common argument, does *not* seem to be a relevant factor. Money is not a scarce resource, it is implied, and "economizing on tax revenues" is hardly important: "Economy in this respect is not equivalent to economy in the administration of the tax system."[11] The individual, who naturally prefers the lower money tax, the argument proceeds, views the situation in terms of an alternative which is not available to all individuals collectively.

The above argument might be objected to by stressing that since to any individual more money *means* more goods, and that the sacrifice he must associate with the payment of taxes *is* the amount of goods and services he could buy at current prices, it is useless, and perhaps even misleading, to attempt to convince him not to prefer that a lower amount of money be taxed away from him (and from everybody else). Certainly, each individual tends to view the problem in terms of alternatives that are not open to all individuals collectively, but that does not nullify the importance of his subjective burdens.

No doubt, a distinction should be drawn between the objective burden, the burden as economists see it, and the "subjective aggregate burden." It should be stressed, however, that the subjective burden is the aggregate burden as perceived by individuals not because they are irrational,* but because they are logical. Trescott suggests the term "fallacies of decomposition" for such attitudes.[12] Yet, while fallacies of compositions are fallacies due to logical pitfalls, the fallacies of decomposition are not fallacies at all from the point of view of those who make them, just as the assumption of perfectly elastic demand that each "pure competitor" makes is not fallacious. If such perceived burdens are, *ceteris paribus*, to be minimized, then the "economic efficiency" of taxation must be of some importance.

However, the importance of this economic efficiency can be proved in purely economic terms. It is true that generalizations of propositions derived for isolated individuals to the community as a whole are often invalid, but a discussion in terms of the economy as a whole has its own pitfalls; for, after all, the economy itself consists of individuals. The argument denying the importance of the economic efficiency of taxation is based on the assumption that money is not a scarce resource, as indeed it is not for the the economy or for the government. But money is definitely a scarce resource for each individual. Utilities of individuals are derived not only from real physical resources, but from money and bonds as

---

* We do not suggest that economists should take into consideration welfare losses of individuals which are due to irrational or mistaken beliefs; how to treat such beliefs must be decided on by politicians. It is for the economists to enlighten the mistaken.

well. And, as Patinkin stresses, money gives utility for individuals not only because it can be spent on goods and services—in which case its utility is only derived—but also because it can be held. Money reserves provide security against financial embarrassment because of lack of synchronization between the inflow and outflow of money in a given period,[13] and if uncertainty is introduced into the argument, as it should be, then the utility supplied by cash balances—precautionary and/or speculative—is greatly enhanced.[14]

The common argument for the case of the economy as a whole neglects the utility of money perhaps because one cannot represent money on a transformation curve. The argument stresses that if two unequal amounts of money taxes are economically equivalent because of compensating differences in "economic efficiency," they both reduce the private resource-using expenditures at the given period to the same extent, which is true by definition, and that, at least if current investment is given, the total potential resource-using expenditures in a future period is also given, which is also true. The conclusion, however, that, *ceteris paribus*, both taxes are equally good (or bad) is wrong, *since the lower money taxes leave the private economy* (all individuals taken together) *with more money balances and/or bonds*.

It should, perhaps, be stressed that the higher money balances that the more "efficient" tax leaves to individuals are also higher real balances, for—and that was the basic assumption—the two alternative taxes are economically equivalent so that the current price level must be the same in both cases. As to bonds, if their present real value is determined by deflating their money value by the present index of the price level, then, since their money value is greater and the price level the same in both cases, the real value left by the more "efficient" tax is also higher than that left by the less "efficient" tax. If bond-owners plan to have them redeemed in a future period and to consume the proceeds, the real value of bonds should, conceptually, be reached by deflating their money value by the price level in that future period. Also, the real amount of resource-using expenditures in that future period depends only on the resources then available, so that, in this case, the aggregate welfare of individuals in that future period does not seem to depend on the amount of their bond-holdings in the present period.* Not all bond-holders, however, plan to redeem all their bonds and to consume all the proceeds. The functions of savings are numerous, and savings cannot therefore be identified with future consumption, an identification which is the essence of the "waiting theory" of interest.[15] Even if one does not agree with Rolph that this theory is "a travesty on the evidence," it is hard to deny that savings do add to individuals' wealth, and that greater wealth not only allows more consumption, but also more security, prestige, and power. To the extent that the function of the bonds is not to provide for future consumption, they might be considered, for the purposes of the problem discussed here, together with money balances. The more "efficient" tax leaves to individuals, collectively, more of either cash balances or bonds or both and, therefore, *ceteris paribus,* the "economy" must be better off. To conclude: the "economic efficiency" of taxation *is* important, and it should be taken into account when choosing between taxes.

Incidentally, since consumption taxes—as partial taxes having both substitution and income effects—are

---

* If debts be considered as negative bond-holdings, the total amount of bond-holdings in a closed economy should, of course, be zero, but not if the debts of the government are not considered negative bond-holdings.

more "efficient" than general income taxes (and this can easily be demonstrated also for the economy as a whole), this point should not be forgotten when a problem such as the "excess-burden-of-indirect-taxes" is discussed. For the case of the economy as a whole, it has been conceded that the excess-burden argument is correct *if*: (a) the partial tax actually does distort the allocation of resources, which is obvious only if the original situation was an optimal one; and if (b) the effects of the partial and the general taxes on the supply of effort are identical. When the welfare implications of the "economic efficiency" of taxation are recognized, these two qualifications are not yet sufficient.

Needless to say, the advantages of the "economic efficiency" of taxation do not imply that more "efficient" taxes should always be preferred. In the case of excises, "economic efficiency" and "excess burden" are inseparable; both are the result of a demand schedule which is somewhat elastic. If the comparative "economic efficiency" of a tax is caused by its comparative regressivity, it should not be forgotten that the less progressive tax indeed leaves to individuals more money balances than does the economically alternative tax. The greater amount of money balances, however, is not left to the very same persons in both cases. Similarly, if two equi-progressive taxes have different "economic efficiency," the disadvantages of the more "efficient" tax—say, distortive effects as defined by the Paretian welfare economics—should be weighed against the advantages of "efficiency."

It should also be remembered that the more savings and less taxes collected—the characteristics of a more "efficient" tax system—mean that the share of the current generation in the output of future periods will be higher than otherwise, which may or may not be desirable. The choice among taxes is always a complicated matter. That, however, does not detract from the importance of all the factors that complicate it.

DEFLATIONARY EFFECTS OF OUTLAY TAXES
AND INCOME TAXES

Those who are not convinced by the argument for the importance of the comparative "economic efficiency" of taxes may note with relief that actual differences between the various taxes in this respect are at the most modest in the long run.

Differences in "efficiency" may be considerable if permanent taxes are compared with temporary ones, or when a tax on permanent incomes is compared with that on temporary incomes. The propensity to consume out of temporary income may be quite low if the effect of that income on the present volume of the expected stream of incomes is relatively negligible.* Otherwise, there may be considerable differences among taxes in the distribution of the resources released between consumption and investment. But it is certainly not clear whether there are important differences in practice in the extent to which alternative taxes have unequal deflationary effects.

It is often assumed that outlay taxes are more deflationary than income taxes that yield equal revenues. The terms "deflationary" or "anti-deflationary" are used here in the meaning of reducing the (posi-

---

* The 1957-58 Survey of Family Savings in Israel established that the propensity to consume—including purchases of consumer durables—was 3.5 times higher for current incomes than for the personal restitution payments received by many citizens. Cf. *Bank of Israel Bulletin*, Vol. 10 (October 1959), pp. 17-41, and esp. pp. 19-21.

This is the major reason why it is often argued that estate taxes and other taxes similar in this respect should be used to finance public investments rather than ordinary public expenditures.

tive) gap between *ex-ante* aggregate demand and *ex-ante* aggregate supply. The common denominator of all taxes whose deflationary effects are compared is that their real yields—their money yield deflated for possible differences in the initial price level—are equal. Such taxes will be referred to hereafter as "equi-revenue taxes."

As the discussion in this context is for the short run, no distinction will be made between resources released by taxation from private consumption and those released from private investment. Because investment increases future output, it is possible that two taxes that are equi-deflationary in the short run are not so in the long run if effects on supply are taken into account.[16]

The belief that outlay taxes are generally more deflationary than income taxes rests on the following allegations: (1) that outlay taxes are comparatively regressive;[17] (2) that outlay taxes raise prices and therefore reduce not only real disposable incomes but real money balances as well;[18] (3) that outlay taxes raise prices but do not affect money disposable income and therefore, through a certain money illusion, are more deflationary than income taxes;[19] (4) that outlay taxes do not discourage saving as do income taxes;[20] and (5) that outlay taxes do not discourage the supply of labor to the same extent as do income taxes.[21]

The standard argument runs as follows: Outlay taxes are usually less progressive than income taxes, and the marginal propensity to consume decreases as income increases; therefore, of two such equi-revenue taxes, the outlay tax will release more resources.

The first major premise—that outlay taxes are less progressive (or more regressive) than income taxes—is derived in part from the observation that outlay taxes are usually imposed on commodities on which expenditure as a percentage of income falls as income rises, and in part from the theoretical assumption that these taxes are shifted forward. The distributional effects of outlay taxes depend, of course, on the shape of the outlay taxes schedule. Some systems of outlay taxes are indeed progressive, even on the assumption of complete forward shifting of "indirect" taxes.[22] However, there is no doubt that outlay taxes imposed on "mass consumption" goods or even general and proportional consumption taxes are regressive in relation to incomes if forward shifting is assumed. Thus the assumption of forward shifting is an integral part of the argument. An excise on bread might be progressive if shifted backward!

We have probably already overstressed the point that forward shifting of a tax may, but does not have to, raise the price level, so that taxes might have been shifted even when usually admitted to be "absorbed." But this argument goes both ways. Partial outlay taxes will be regressive if the supply of the production factors used in producing the taxed goods is highly elastic so that the taxes are shifted to consumers for whom spending on the taxed items as a percentage of income happens to decline with income, or—if this is not the case—if those factors of production that happen to suffer are relatively poor.

The second major premise of the standard argument that attributes stronger deflationary effects to outlay taxes than to income taxes is that the marginal propensity to consume declines as income rises. Actually, if the purpose of the government is to release resources not only from private consumption but from private use, what is relevant is the marginal propensity to spend, not the marginal propensity to consume. Even if the marginal propensity to consume decreases somewhat as income rises, the marginal propensity to spend, that is, to consume and to invest, might behave quite differently.

As a matter of fact, it is not established that the marginal propensity to consume does vary from one level of disposable income[23] to another. Consumer budget studies in the United States and the United Kingdom have often been interpreted as indicating a nearly uniform marginal propensity to consume over the range in which most income is earned. This statistical conclusion depends, of course, on the kind of function fitted, and there might be a "natural bias" towards a linear function. On the other hand, even if "cross-section" data do indicate a marginal propensity to consume diminishing with income, redistribution of incomes will not necessarily affect the total volume of consumption. The members of one income group may differ from those of another in such respects as taste, age, family size, occupational distribution, functional distribution of income, urban-rural distribution, the proportion of transitory to permanent incomes, and the interest rates at which they can borrow or lend. Such differences might so influence the average propensity to consume that the statistical consumption function yielded by the data would be convex, although the points that determined it really lay on linear and perhaps even parallel income consumption curves.

Such possible differences between income groups are of special importance in determining the comparative deflationary effects of taxes that are not equally progressive when the differences themselves are the results of progressive elements in taxation. Kaldor, for example, puts a strong stress on the disincentive effects on savings of highly progressive income taxes, which sharply reduce the net interest return of the rich.[24] Such arguments have always been opposed by the supposition that savings are rather insensitive to changes in interest rates. But as Kaldor notes, the range of *net* interest rates is much greater than the range of historical variation of the "pure" long-term rate of interest over the last hundred years or so. The assumption of decreasing marginal propensity to consume should therefore be replaced by the more controversial assumption that, even when the substitution effects of both taxes are taken into account, the "corrected" marginal propensity to spend—that is, simply the decrease in total spending divided by the sum paid in taxes—declines as income rises.

The argument that outlay taxes are more deflationary than income taxes (because they are less progressive) also rests on the additional assumption that the less progressive of two equi-revenue taxes does not reduce *ex-ante* aggregate supply by more than does the more progressive tax. (For, to repeat, the deflationary effects of a tax are defined and measured here in terms of its quantitative effects on the inflationary *gap*.) This latter assumption is reasonable, however, since it can be demonstrated that the more progressive a tax is, the more adverse are its effects on the supplies of effort and risk-taking. All in all, if there is a big difference between the distributional impact of two equi-revenue taxes, the more progressive tax would probably be the less deflationary. But the differences in deflationary effects might be smaller than is ordinarily expected.

The argument claiming stronger deflationary effects for outlay taxes than for more progressive income taxes yielding the same revenue is independent of what happens to the absolute price level. Some other arguments to the same effect are not. They will be examined now.

E. Cary Brown, whose main thesis will be discussed later, mentions the following two arguments as supporting the superiority of outlay taxes as deflationary fiscal tools:

(a) If consumption taxes raise the general level of prices, as assumed, and if the quantity of money remains constant, the added demand for money for transactions, in the absence of a counterbalancing reduction in demand for it in other directions, would raise interest rates. . . . The principal effect of higher interest rates would be to discourage investment.[25] (b) Higher prices induced by consumption taxes would reduce the value of real wealth (given a constant stock of money). If consumption depends on real wealth as well as on real income, real consumption would fall. . . . This . . . would work in favor of greater deflation from consumption taxes.[26]

Both arguments rest on somewhat inconsistent assumptions. For one, Cary Brown explicitly assumes that the general price level is raised by the consumption taxes and that the supply of money is unchanged. But something besides prices must have been changed. If increases in velocity are ruled out, real balance effects of outlay taxes cannot exist, for if money balances are unchanged, the price level will also be unchanged; if money balances are increased, the price level will indeed rise, and to the same extent, but real balances will not fall at all. If there is some increase in the velocity of circulation, and as we have seen there might be, it is not made clear *why* it takes place or why it would necessarily not take place with other taxes.

The same comments apply to Brown's main thesis[27] —that is, that "money illusion" could be a reason for comparatively stronger deflationary effects of outlay taxes. "Money illusion," which essentially involves a failure to grasp the true relationships between the real and the monetary spheres, has no standard definition. At best, it has become a sort of *deus ex machina,* the purpose of which is to explain the incomprehensible.

Gardiner C. Means, for example, defines "money illusion" in the consumers' goods markets as existing *if*, when consumers' real incomes remain constant but dollar incomes and prices fall, real consumer expenditures increase, presumably because prices seem lower.[28] To Ta-Chung Liu and Ching Gwan Chang, Means's definition is that of "money *price* illusion." They define, on the other hand, "money *income* illusion"—that is, when, with real income constant but money income and prices falling proportionately, people are led by the smaller money income to believe that they are "poorer" and hence to consume less.[29] The implication of "money *income* illusion" is the opposite of that of "money *price* illusion," and vice versa (*ibid.*). And if both are of similar frequency and strength, there will be no "money illusion" at all.

According to Cary Brown, "money illusion" in the market for commodities means that "money expenditures depend solely on money disposable income." That is, "a consumer with a fixed dollar income is regarded as spending a fixed number of dollars on consumption, regardless of the level of prices."[30] Such a consumption function involves "money illusion" only if the marginal propensity to consume is not equal at relevant income levels to the average propensity to consume, for otherwise real consumption is always the same proportion of real income and money consumption is always the same proportion of money income.

Obviously, if various "money illusions" are arbitrarily assumed, any conclusion can be reached. For example, Lawrence S. Ritter believes in a "money illusion" that implies that real consumption depends upon disposable money income.[31] If so, income taxes should be much more deflationary than outlay taxes!

It is because of such confusion that one wishes for some elaboration of the causes of Brown's kind of "money illusion." It would seem that the typical con-

sumer—a housewife who does not even keep accounts
—would not necessarily stop consuming, once a certain amount of money was expended. It should also
be noted that this "illusion" is made to order to fit
the case of an imposition of outlay taxes; for where
else could one assume for the whole economy, excluding the government, a fixed dollar income and a changing level of prices?

Briefly, Brown's argument is as follows: By definition, a consumer who suffers from "Brown's money illusion" spends a fixed amount of money on consumption out of a fixed dollar income, regardless of the level
of prices. Thus the imposition of a proportional consumption tax, which is assumed to raise prices for consumers, instead of a proportional income tax that yields
the same money revenue, will lower real consumption if the marginal propensity to consume out of disposable money income is less than unity. Let us suppose that before either of these two taxes was imposed,
there were no government expenditures, and that
money (and real) income, equal to money (and real)
disposable income,* was at a level of $100. Let us fur-
ther suppose that consumption expenditures were $90
and savings (and investment) $10, in which case a
proportional income tax at a rate of 10 per cent would
yield $10. If the marginal propensity to consume out of
disposable money income was, say, 0.7, consumption
would fall to $83 (and savings to $7). An alternative
proportional consumption tax, which is shifted completely forward, would not change disposable money
income as compared with the situation in which no
taxes were imposed, and, because of "Brown's money
illusion," money outlay on consumption would therefore remain at $90. But, since the consumption tax is

* That is, if there are no corporate savings and taxes. See
Cary Brown, "Consumption Taxes and Income Determination,"
American Economic Review, Vol. XL (March 1950), p. 77n.

assumed to be shifted fully in higher prices for consumers and since it is assumed to yield a revenue equal to that of the income tax, the consumption tax would reduce money consumers' outlays measured in pre-tax prices to $80, that is, exactly by the amount of tax collected.

In other words, if "Brown's money illusion" exists, the marginal propensity to consume out of real disposable income, when disposable real income (but not disposable money income) declines, is unity.

Besides his specific money-illusion assumption, Brown's major assumption is that the consumption tax is shifted fully in higher absolute prices for consumers, so that the tax causes no change in disposable money income as compared with the pre-tax situation. This assumption can be interpreted in various ways, the first, and simplest, of which is that the supply of money or its velocity of circulation is increased. In this case it does not matter whether the outlay tax is partial or general. The second interpretation, which excludes any increase in the money supply, is that the absolute rise in the prices of consumer goods is accompanied by an absolute fall in the prices of capital goods, so no change occurs in the average price level.

If the outlay tax is "shifted" fully in higher prices because the money supply is expanded, then the extra deflationary effects that Brown attributes to the outlay tax should be attributed instead to the expansion in money supply. To be sure, when the price level rises (for monetary reasons), outlay taxes can prevent disposable money income from rising with the price level and thus create a situation in which "Brown's money illusion" might work. *But this could be achieved just as well by income taxes.* Brown's argument illustrates, in short, a possible deflationary effect of inflation. That there are "deflationary aspects of inflation" is rather well known.[32]

The second interpretation of Brown's argument stresses the partiality of his consumption taxes. Surely, even with constant money supply, consumption taxes may be fully shifted forward in higher absolute prices if the prices of capital goods (the nontaxed goods) decline so that no change occurs in the absolute price level. But if that is what Brown's argument assumes, all that is proved is that consumption taxes release more resources from private consumption than do general income taxes. This, however, is too obvious. A discriminating tax has the same income effects as an equi-revenue general tax, but it also has substitution effects. If the government is interested in releasing specific resources from private use, discriminating taxes will require less revenues than will nondiscriminating taxes—and Brown's consumption tax is, of course, a discriminating tax. All this, however, has very little to do with the deflationary effects of taxes, which include the effects on the demand for (and the supply of) all resources. Every discrimination *against* something is also a discrimination *in favor* of something else.

As previously noted, Brown's consumption function need not involve "money illusion" at all. Briefly, his "illusionless" argument is that, if the marginal propensity to save is equal at all relevant income levels to the average propensity to save, a consumer will spend the same number of dollars before and after the imposition of price-raising consumption taxes. In that case, since real saving is always the same proportion of real income, the reduction in real savings—a reduction which must take place when disposable real income is reduced by the consumption taxes—occurs when money savings (and consumption) do not decline at all.[33]

The equivalence of the argument to that of "Brown's money illusion" is complete when equality of the average and marginal propensities to save is assumed. But even in other cases, by virtue of the increased cost of living, an unchanged quantity of money saving will have a diminished value in real terms. Consequently, part of the needed reduction in real saving takes place even if money saving does not decline, and a reduction in money saving smaller than that indicated by the marginal propensity to save will suffice to produce the required reduction in real saving.

The "illusionless" argument also requires either the assumption of increased money supply or the assumption of the partiality of the taxes imposed. Moreover, this time the assumption of partiality alone does not suffice. Implicitly, it is also assumed here that real savings are money savings deflated by the cost-of-living index, that is, by an index of the prices of consumer goods. (The corollary of this assumption is that outlay taxes on investment goods do not affect the value of real savings or, more exactly, increase it by shifting resources from investment to consumption!) Just what price index should be applied to money savings is an awkward problem indeed, and the answer to it will vary according to the functions of savings.

Note also that since consumption taxes are discriminatory taxes not imposed on investment goods, the rate of the consumption taxes must, because of the lower tax base, be higher than that of an equi-revenue proportional income tax if they are to yield equal revenues. "Disposable real income,"—that is, disposable money income deflated by a price index representing the new price level of consumer goods—will therefore be lower than disposable money (and real) income when the equi-revenue income tax is collected. If so, the argument, which again rests on a sort of an illusion, although a more understandable one than "Brown's money illusion," is quite obvious.

As already noted, the deflationary effects of taxes which are the result of exempting savings or investments in the form of an expenditure tax (*à la* Kaldor) or of a sales tax will clearly release more resources from consumption than would a more general tax that yielded an equal revenue. As to effects on the supply of effort, there is no analytical presumption that one category of taxes is superior to another. It all depends on the rate-structure progression of the tax as applied to incomes from effort.

To sum up, the economic "efficiency" of taxation is of importance since it affects the taxpayers' psychic welfare. This is not to say, however, that it could ever serve as a *single* criterion for tax policy. The taxation of rich misers, for example, is often functionless, but even in spite of rational judgments to the contrary, few would agree to exempt them from taxation. This example may seem strange, but in a way the whole category of death taxes bears a strong resemblance to a tax on rich misers—and yet would you vote to eliminate them from the tax system?

As a matter of fact the very belief that the economic "efficiency" of such taxes is low may be quite mistaken. To the extent that such taxes pacify labor, they may be quite important in delaying or moderating demands for wage increases which under a wage standard will lead to inflation. Estate taxes, excess profits taxes, to some extent property taxes and other taxes on capital may under the circumstances play a deflationary role which is hardly related to their revenues. This applies as well to the notoriously high marginal rates of income taxes at the top income-brackets.

In any case, tax "efficiency" is never a single goal; it is only one among other, often much more important, goals.

NOTES

1. Cf. Abba P. Lerner, *The Economics of Control* (London: Macmillan, 1941), p. 308.

2. Nicholas Kaldor, *An Expenditure Tax* (London: Allen & Unwin, 1955), p. 175.

3. *Ibid.*, pp. 173-75.

4. Carl S. Shoup, "Taxation and Fiscal Policy," in *Income Stabilization for a Developing Democracy*, ed. by Max F. Millikan (New Haven, Connecticut: Yale University Press, 1953), p. 267.

5. Cf. George F. Break, in his review of Kaldor's *An Expenditure Tax Economica*, Vol. XXIII (May 1956), p. 177.

6. Cf. James Tobin, "Taxes, Saving and Inflation," *American Economic Review*, Vol. XXXIX (December 1949), pp. 1223-32, esp. p. 1229.

7. Cf. M. F. W. Joseph, "The Excess Burden of Indirect Taxation," *Review of Economic Studies*, Vol. VI (June 1939), pp. 226-31.

8. Cf. David Walker, "The Direct-Indirect Tax Problem: Fifteen Years of Controversy," *Public Finance*, Vol. X, No. 2 (1955), pp. 153-76.

9. See Richard A. Musgrave, *The Theory of Public Finance* (New York: McGraw-Hill, 1959), pp. 155-57.

10. Earl R. Rolph, *The Theory of Fiscal Economics* (Berkeley, Calif.: University of California Press, 1954), p. 53.

11. See G. F. Break, *op. cit.*, p. 177.

12. Cf. Paul Trescott, "The Burdens of Government Finance," *Public Finance*, Vol. XI, No. 2 (1956), pp. 164-76.

13. Don Patinkin, *Money, Interest, and Prices* (Evans-

ton, Illinois: Row, Peterson, 1956), Chaps. V, VI, esp. pp. 62-64.

14. Cf. J. C. Gilbert, "The Demand for Money: The Development of an Economic Concept," *Journal of Political Economy*, Vol. LXI (April 1953), pp. 144-59.

15. See Earl R. Rolph, *op. cit.*, pp. 262-65. Rolph notes that his ideas lean heavily upon those of the late Henry Simons.

16. See Arthur Smithies, "The Control of Inflation," *Review of Economics and Statistics*, Vol. XXXIX (August 1957), pp. 272-83.

17. See Richard A. Musgrave and Mary S. Painter, "The Impact of Alternative Tax Structures on Personal Consumption and Savings," *Quarterly Journal of Economics*, Vol. LXII (August 1948), pp. 475-99.

18. See E. Cary Brown, "Consumption Taxes and Income Determination," *American Economic Review*, Vol. XL (March 1950), pp. 74-89.

19. *Ibid.*, pp. 130-40; see also William H. White, "Measuring the Inflationary Significance of a Government Budget," *International Monetary Fund Staff Papers*, Vol. I, pp. 362-63.

20. See Nicholas Kaldor, *An Expenditure Tax, op. cit.*, pp. 79-101.

21. *Ibid.*, pp. 76-81.

22. See Richard Goode, "Report of the Indian Taxation Enquiry Commission," *National Tax Journal*, Vol. IX (June 1956), p. 136; and "The Effects of the Norwegian Tax System on the Personal Income Distribution,"*Statistick Sentralbyra* (Oslo, 1954), pp. 93-94.

23. See Cary Brown, *op. cit.*, pp. 75-76; Goode, *op. cit.*, pp. 150-51; H. Lubell, "Effects of Redistribution of Income on Consumers' Expenditures," *American Economic Review*, Vol. XXXVII (March 1947), pp. 157-70; Musgrave and Painter, *op. cit.*, pp. 475-99.

24. See Kaldor, *op. cit.*, pp. 91-96.

25. See Cary Brown, *op. cit.*, pp. 85-86.

26. *Ibid.*, p. 86.

27. See also William H. White, "Measuring the Inflationary Significance of a Government Budget," *International Monetary Fund Staff Papers*, Vol. I (April 1951), esp. pp. 362-63; Richard Goode, "Anti-Inflationary Implications of Alternative Forms of Taxation," *American Economic Review*, Vol. XLII (May 1951), p. 156.

28. Gardner C. Means, "Consumption and Investment Propensities: Comment," *American Economic Review*, Vol. XLVIII (March 1953), p. 146.

29. Ta-Chung Liu and Ching Gwan Chang, "Consumption and Investment Propensities: Rejoinder," *American Economic Review*, Vol. XLVIII (March 1953), p. 149.

30. Cary Brown, *op. cit.*, pp. 74-89. This consumption function is also assumed by Ralph Turvey in his "Some Notes on Multiplier Theory," *American Economic Review*, Vol. XLIII (June 1953), p. 280.

31. Lawrence S. Ritter, "Consumption Taxes and Income Determination: Comment," *American Economic Review*, Vol. XLI (March 1951), pp. 191-93.

32. See Milton Friedman, "Discussion of the Inflationary Gap," in *Essays in Positive Economics* (Chicago: University of Chicago Press, 1953), pp. 251-62. For a discussion of deflationary effects of public debt operations, see Earl R. Rolph, "The Incidence of Public Debt Operations," *National Tax Journal*, Vol. IX (December 1956), pp. 339-53; see also Rolph's "Principles of Debt Management," *American Economic Review*, Vol. XLVII (June 1957), pp. 302-20.

33. Cf. White, *op. cit.*, p. 362.

CHAPTER FOUR

ON PROGRESSIVE
TAXATION

Progressive taxation is a main fiscal instrument of the redistributive branch of Public Finance. Yet the various quasi-scientific rationalizations of progressive taxation—the benefit principle from the point of view of that branch, and the three sacrifice approaches: the equal sacrifice, the equi-proportionate sacrifice, and the minimum sacrifice approach—have proved either too little or too much, and are therefore inadequate and superfluous at the same time. Since all arguments for and against progressive taxation have been brilliantly re-examined rather recently,[1] there is not much sense in rediscussing them here, especially since I believe that the best justification for progressive taxation is the social value judgment, if it exists, that it is good taxation. Basically, this is the opinion of the late Henry C. Simons.

> The case for drastic progression in taxation must be rested on the case against inequality—on the ethical or aesthetic judgement that the prevailing distribution of wealth reveals a degree (and/or kind) of inequality which is distinctly evil or unlovely.[2]

The main disadvantage of this aproach is, of course, that it convinces only those who need no proof. But there are other problems as well. Any value judgment presupposes that there is no dispute as to the contents of what is judged. Yet the meaning of progressive taxation is, as we intend to demonstrate, not at all as clear as it is supposed to be.

Since the case for progressive taxation rests upon the case against inequality of incomes and wealth, a progressive tax, that is, a redistributive tax, should be by definition a tax that helps society to achieve a less unequal distribution of income. Obviously, the first difficulty arises from the possible ambiguity of the very change in the distribution of income. Simons's judgment that the prevailing distribution of income is evil does not provide us with a standard for one which is desirable. Suppose the pre-tax and post-tax Lorenz curves of income distribution intersect each other, as they might and sometimes do.[3] It is always possible, of course, to devise some coefficients of equality that will produce definite answers, but such answers will not necessarily be socially meaningful.

> The degree of departure from absolute equality, however measured or stated, must itself be referred, if not

explicitly, then in some vague way, to a standard of normal or justifiable concentration. . . .[4]

If "the amount of concentration, the amount of departure from a condition of uniform incomes, does not matter so much as does the particular form of the income distribution underlying the concentration,"[5] then a change in income distribution which is "progressive" by the verdict of "coefficients of equality" might still be a change in the wrong direction.

This point should not be overstated. Yet it is important to realize that the principle of progressivity in taxation should be supplemented, at least occasionally, with some other principles, even if only the distribution aspects of taxation are considered. Indeed, the standard of normal or justifiable concentration of incomes, by which one should judge the distributional effects of taxation, is probably very much influenced by what is done with income by people in various income brackets.[6]

THE TIME DIMENSION OF PROGRESSIVITY

Most conceptual difficulties of progressive taxation are derived from the difficulties of the meaning of a change towards equality in the distribution of income. Another difficulty is that this change itself cannot be timeless. Is the intention to modify the distribution of income by brackets, immediately, or perhaps in the short run, or maybe in the long run? This is not an easy question to answer, even if the number of households in the economy is assumed to be constant, as is perfect foresight. The "immediate" distribution of observed incomes is their distribution in the shortest period for which there are statistical data, say, a year. But the long-run distribution of incomes will reflect aggregations for each household of incomes received or to be received in all periods—past, present, or future—with incomes in any future period being discounted according to the relevant discount factors which differ according to circumstances and the length of waiting involved. The long-run distribution of incomes is thus the distribution of wealth, while the short-run distribution of incomes reflects a partial aggregation of incomes in some necessarily arbitrary time period longer than the shortest period for which there is data.

The long-run distribution of incomes, even under our assumptions, will be different in each year in which it is computed due to changes in the interest rate. For the poor fellow who cannot borrow against his future incomes, the future may rightly seem very, very far away. Still, under the circumstances, it is clearly the long-run distribution of income which should be the main policy variable. The very recognition, which is quite general, that some sort of averaging of incomes over time is needed when an income tax with a progressive rate structure is imposed on incomes that are realized in big lumps rather than continuously seems to imply that the goal of redistributive taxation is not an immediate effect on the distribution of income; otherwise, no averaging would be needed.

But the long-run income distribution has many problematic aspects, even under the unnatural demographic assumptions used here to simplify matters. First, it should be clear that effects of fiscal (or monetary) measures on the distribution of income might be different in the "three runs." It is often argued, and indeed follows from the premises, that if the marginal private propensity to save rises with "immediate" observed income, and if the government has a low, if positive at all, propensity to save, progressive taxation in the "immediate run" will decrease savings and thus, other things being equal, decelerate the rate of capital accumulation and ultimately lower the future average real income below a level that could otherwise have been possible. Given the basic assumptions, this should happen as a result of the effect of progressive taxation on the size and distribution of private purchasing-power, even if such taxation has no substitution effects unfavorable to savings. The effects of progressive taxation (in the "immediate" sense) on the size of future national income will not, however, be discussed here. Increased production and increased distributional equity are often competing goals in tax policy, yet this competition makes neither of the two less important or less clear. It is up to society to decide whether the cost at the margin in terms of future production and other costs of increased distributional justice does or does not exceed the price it is ready to pay for it. Moreover, this particular dilemma is a necessary one, given the assumptions only under pure private capitalism, that is, where the government does not participate or even intentionally interfere with the investment process. Obviously, if the proceeds of taxation—however progressive it might be—are invested, the rate of capital formation will be accelerated, not decelerated.

As Samuelson has noted, direct investment by the government is not the only solution to the capital-formation vs. distributional equity dilemma; for, say, by means of a low-interest monetary policy, a highly progressive tax system and a surplus budget, "a community can have full employment and it can at the same time have the rate of capital formation it wants and it can accomplish all this compatibly with the degree of income distribution it ethically desires."[7] In any case, the point to be stressed here is a different one. A smaller than otherwise capital stock implies a higher than otherwise marginal productivity of capital, and this might have effects not only on the size of national income but also on the distribution of income by size as well as on the distribution of income by factor shares. If conflict does arise, not only between progressivity and other goals of taxation, but also between progressivity in the short run and progressivity in the long run, then lenient income-tax treatment for savings, for example, is not necessarily nonprogressive even if income is defined to include savings.

Until now the discussion has intentionally abstracted from some complicating factors. But when the actualities of demographic growth (and decline) are introduced, the long-run distribution of incomes becomes much more obscure. It makes little sense, for example, to include in the distribution the "assessed" incomes of as-yet unborn children, even if adequately discounted. Besides, if, say, because of technological innovation, incomes per capita tend to rise from year to year, it is not clear that such growth—which will make future generations richer—should not be incorporated into the discount factor so that future incomes should be discounted more heavily not because they are future incomes but on grounds of diminishing marginal utility.*

This, incidentally, raises interesting problems in the intergenerations fiscal equity. For instance, there is no reason why the principles of ability to pay should apply only to intrageneration differences in wealth. If an annual rate of growth of 2 to 3 per cent in the average income per person may be taken for granted, average incomes will grow in thirty years by 81 to 143 per cent. It is currently recognized that facilities provided for by the government will be used frequently by several generations of taxpayers, and therefore loan

---

* Cf. Otto Eckstein, "A Survey of the Theory of Public Expenditures Criteria," in *Public Finances: Needs, Sources, and Utilization* (Princeton, N.J.: Princeton University Press, 1961), pp. 453-60, and the comment by Jack Hirshleifer, *ibid.,* pp. 495-96.

finance is required to permit benefit taxation. But does it not follow that the next generation, being richer, should pay more than its proportional share in the benefits (as measured by costs)? In this era where growth is applauded, is it sacrilegious to suggest that, in countries where incomes are already relatively high, the next generation should pay a share of the public expenditures for current benefits, that is, by reducing the rate of growth itself? If the answer is yes, there is a good case to be made for financing more current expenditures by borrowing from the public.[8]

PARTIAL PROGRESSIVITY

Various taxes, or even some details in tax laws, are often criticized as regressive. But even if the purpose of progressive taxation is to redistribute real income more equally, it does not follow that all its components should be progressive. Indeed, there are many ways of achieving a given change in the distribution of income. We shall refer to the set of tax systems which bring about a certain change in income distribution as an equi-distributive set. And if the expenditure side of the budget is included in the picture, as it should be, equi-distributive systems are fiscal systems that on the whole bring about a given change in income distribution.[9] Between equi-distributive sets, to say the obvious, one can choose on any ground but their distributional effects.

Suppose the "will of society" has been determined and it is to move Lorenz curve *A* to Lorenz curve *B*, which represents a less unequal income distribution. If the distributional effects of government expenditures are abstracted from, taxation should be progressive; yet it may also include many regressive elements. To criticize such regressive elements because of their regressivity would, in this case, be to disagree with "the will of society." True, it is useful to know how the final outcome is brought about—that is, what are the progressive and what are the regressive elements in the system—but it is important to bear in mind that these "conflicting" elements are part and parcel of an equi-progressive taxation set. Exemption of interest on state or local bonds, accelerated depreciation, percentage depletion, and the like might be regressive, but if they are undesirable it is not due to their regressivity. For, if these special features of the system are abolished, other features must be made less progressive. Conversely, if the critic is unhappy with the level of progressivity, a higher level can be reached by many other ways—say, by steepening the progression of the rates. Economists rarely criticize a rate structure because it is not "progressive" enough, since they usually realize that such a criticism would involve an implicit value judgment. Yet to criticize, say, accelerated depreciation on distributional grounds is also an expression of a value judgment.

Interestingly enough, much political energy is expended in all countries on discussing, in terms of their distributional effects, some tax features which can be easily offset by many other tax details. One such discussion is that of the merits and demerits of tax credits for dependents vs. tax deductions (or exemptions). To insist on tax credits instead of exemptions or deductions in order to get rid of a regressive element in a progressive tax, which is one (although a very important one) of many taxes some of which are highly regressive, is no more "logical" than to argue for a "regressive rate structure" in order to turn the exemptions or personal deductions into "progressive" components of the system.

As a matter of fact, even from a purely distributional point of view, the advantages of tax credits are not very clear. When exemptions or deductions are used, the balance of the tax paid by a bachelor over the tax paid by a head of a family earning the same income rises as income rises. This seems to be right and proper, for the purpose of exemptions, deductions, or tax credits is to make allowance for differences in ability to pay caused by differences in the numbers of dependents. Yet this increasing-with-incomes excess on a bachelor is only a mirror reflection of the alleged regressivity of tax exemptions which depends on the rising-with-incomes-tax savings through exemptions or deductions.* Even if deductions were clearly inferior on distributional grounds, this would not be a decisive factor against them unless very little could be argued in their favor. Accelerated depreciation is basically a reduction in taxes for people who invest in depreciable assets; but if efficient in terms of its goals it might be a good policy to follow even if it in itself reduces over-all tax progressivity. Exemption of imputed rent from income tax is to be resented, but not because it probably reduces the progressivity of the income tax; even a contrary policy—that is, exemptions from income tax for paid rents and nonexemption for imputed rents, which needless to say, would have different distributional effects—should be resented on nondistributional grounds.

The concept of "equi-distributive" fiscal sets might provide a framework for a truly economic analysis of alternative tax systems. On the matter of choice between nonequi-distributive sets, the economist, as an economist, has little valuable to say. If, however, the desired over-all impact on the distribution of income is explicitly specified, he should be able to advise tax

---

* I owe this point, and a clarification of the whole problem of tax credits vs. tax reductions, to Mr. Yoram Haroé, who stresses that deductions for dependents are not subsidies, reductions, or other deviations from the principle of "ability to pay." On the contrary, if no deductions (or tax credits) were given for dependents, bachelors would get an unjustified tax abatement.

legislators on the economic way to achieve this aim, such as, the roles that should be played by direct and indirect taxes, and the best structure of each. Certainly it is legitimate to ask whether the degree of progressivity achieved by some tax systems could not also be achieved by somewhat less progressive income taxes and somewhat more progressive outlay taxes, and whether on grounds other than those of equity such an alternative system might not be superior.

The "partial progressivity" approach towards separate taxes is misleading not only because it is illegitimate to judge details of the fiscal system according to criteria which are relevant only to the system as a whole, but also because some supposedly progressive elements in the fiscal system might render the total system less progressive than otherwise. This might happen if the use of some "progressive components" in the fiscal system decreases its revenue potential. Suppose that the progressivity of an income tax decreases its capacity as a revenue producer compared to, say, a proportional income tax; suppose also that a regressive excise is imposed, so that the regressive excise and the progressive income tax will bring in the same tax revenues that the proportional income tax could have produced alone. In what sense is the progressive tax progressive?

All this is hypothetical, to be sure, yet it is important. The income tax is the strongest element of progressivity in most tax systems, and when its capacity is reached, new taxes imposed will hardly be as progressive, if not actually regressive. Since government expenditures in practice are always higher than the revenues from income tax and resort is taken to other taxes, it is relevant and important to ask whether the progressivity of the income tax decreases or increases its capacity as a revenue producer.

Opinions differ on this matter. With respect to the

excess profits tax, for example, some economists have argued that "a proportional levy yields less revenue than a progressive one,"[10] while others have said that progressive taxation obviously implies a sacrifice for the Treasury.[11] These contradicting views refer to progression in the rate structure. Those who believe that a progressive income tax yields more money than a proportional income tax stress the purchasing-power effects of taxation: they argue that the government cannot and should not impose tax rates on the lower income groups which will push them below the subsistence level. And, indeed, very few government expenditures are important enough to justify cutting into the low standards of living of the very poor. Since a proportional tax would impose a rather low rate on everyone, dictated by the purchasing-power effects of the tax on low income groups, its taxable capacity would thus be lower than that of a progressive levy. The opposite view stresses the substitution effects of taxation. There must be a certain high marginal rate beyond which the substitution effects of taxation offset its anti-inflationary purchasing-power effects through their influence on incentives to effort and spending. Since this maximum rate, if imposed at all, must—where there are quite a few income brackets and where marginal rates rise from one bracket to another —be limited to the very highest income groups, lower (but still very high!) income groups will pay a lower rate—although they could have paid more in the sense that the sacrifices, both private and social, involved in their paying more would have been less than the sacrifices imposed by the most costly existing taxes that could otherwise have been abolished.

The question whether progression increases or decreases the capacity of an income tax cannot be answered *a priori*. But certainly capacity would be at its highest were progression less steep and were only a few marginal rates imposed: a low rate on low income groups, where the purchasing-power effects are dominant as the limiting factor; a high rate, determined by undesirable substitution effects, on high and very high incomes; and possibly another rate in-between. Such an income tax would be much less progressive in itself than one with almost continuously rising marginal rates. Yet this conclusion does not necessarily hold true if this latter tax is not the only one in the fiscal system; in a way its very progressivity may be at least partially responsible for the concomitant use of other much less progressive taxes.

Indeed, a quick progression in rates might turn the income tax itself into a less progressive fiscal instrument if this very progression necessitates special treatment of some kinds of income. As long as averaging of incomes for tax purposes is considered to be beyond the administrative ability of the internal revenue office, the exemption or lenient tax treatment of real capital gains, for instance, is best defended by referring to the progression in the rates and the lumpy nature of such incomes. In other words, the case for taxing capital gains differently from other kinds of income would be much weaker were the rate structure proportional. The trouble is that even a proportional rate imposed only on capital gains would apparently make a good progressive tax. Nor are capital gains the only example. To a large extent the same is true of corporate savings. Because of the progression in the rate structure of the individual income tax, corporate savings are not ordinarily taxed according to the "partnership method," that is, according to each shareholder's ability to pay.

Let us add that if progression tends to narrow the tax base, then it also tends to diminish the "surplus" or "rent" element in the tax payment. As already noted, if a definition of income for tax purposes could possibly include psychological "income" from leisure and liquidity as well as money income from whatever source, there would be almost no way to avoid the tax; it would have no announcement or substitutions effects. But such a definition of income is obviously impractical for tax purposes. We mention it here only to stress the importance of a broad definition of the tax base. The importance of an exemption of capital gains, for instance, does not rest solely on the abatement granted to those who have real capital gains, but also, if not mainly, on the possibilities of either "translating" other incomes into capital gains or of directing resources towards activities with prospects of capital gains. These possibilities, however, are not open to the same extent to all income groups. Worse still, such possibilities not only reduce the tax revenues, but, by means of their allocational effects, reduce the tax capacity and thus may either create a good cause for a reduction in the progression of rates in the income tax itself, or bring about certain (or more extensive) use of some less progressive tax, or abolish (or decrease) some government expenditures which might be especially beneficial to the poor. Progressive taxation is a relative concept, and the results of the comparison of the distributions of income depend, naturally, on the kind of comparisons made. Which ones *are* truly relevant is not always clear.

Take first a kind of a repressed inflation where a relatively bigger gap obtains in the commodity market than in the factor market, in the sense that actual prices are relatively further below equilibrium prices in the former than in the latter. Suppose the government attempts to close the gaps by imposing indirect taxes both on commodities and on employment. In many circumstances such a policy would be reasonable. But would it be progressive? The tax on employment, completely absorbed by employers in a regime of rigid price controls, is probably a progressive tax. Yet the indirect taxes on commodities might be truly regressive, for backward shifting is improbable under conditions of excess-demand for the factors of production. In short, the progressivity of the policy as a whole depends on the relative importance of the progressive and regressive elements. In our case, however, the regressive elements may predominate for, as assumed, there is a greater disequilibrium in the commodity market than in the factor market. But a greater disequilibrium in the commodity market means that when the prices of commodities and of wages were arbitrarily fixed by the authorities, the real tax imposed on employers in the form of controlled prices was relatively higher than that imposed on employees. In other words, if the distortion of the wage-price relationship caused by repressed inflation is progressive, then the remedy to this distortion must by itself be regressive. A progressive fiscal system cannot offset, so to speak, "progressive" distortions. But distortions, progressive or not, have to be cancelled. This is not to say that a mistake has been made in indicating the over-all regressive element in the scheme to close the gap with taxes, but it should have been clear from the very beginning that the gaps themselves have distributional impacts.

A second example illustrating a possible "pitfall" is that of a custom duty imposed on a commodity the imports of which are regulated by an effective quota; that is, the amount demanded of this commodity at world prices and at the current (fixed) official exchange rate exceeds the amount supplied—the quota. Such a custom duty, if it is not higher than the difference between world prices in local currency and the local equilibrium price, will not raise prices at all but will instead reduce the excessive profits of the importers. This reflects the basic proposition that assumptions about tax incidence must precede any distributional analysis.

Or take the case of a planned inflation. In the hope that inflation will transfer resources to the high income groups and thus, if the marginal propensity to save increases with income, increase savings, a deliberate inflation might be attempted. In the absence of an income tax, the amount of income to be transferred from consumers to private investors is determined by the level of the desired investment and the investors' marginal propensity to invest. If businessmen tend to invest a quarter of any increase in their incomes, these incomes will have to be increased by four times the amount of the investment target. But if there is a marginal income tax of, say, 50 per cent on these incomes, the increase in the income of profit-receivers would have to be eight times the investment target; were the rate 75 per cent, the increase would have to be sixteen times the target. Thus the more progressive the income tax, the greater the required transfer of income from the "poor" to the "rich," or, alternatively, the more regressive the entire fiscal policy that will be required if the investment targets are to be reached through private investment.

The lesson of this example is probably only too clear; it makes no sense to follow two contradictory policies at the same time. A more equal distribution of income either is a policy target or it isn't. If it isn't, but if lip service continues to be paid to it in the form of a progressive tax, no improvement in the distribution of income will occur.

PROGRESSIVITY, PROGRESSION, AND "MORALS"

While we are on the subject, it might be helpful to distinguish between progressivity and progression.[12] The two terms are not synonymous. A rise in the average tax rate when the tax base rises is a necessary property of progression, but it has no intrinsic relationship with progressive taxation, that is, redistributive taxation. For example, if the tax base is the number of dependents in the taxpayer's family or the number of loaves of bread consumed, then obviously the quicker the progression of the rates, the greater the regressivity of the tax in the substantial, rather than technical, meanings of the word.[13]

Truly, a tax system cannot be progressive unless the percentage of incomes paid in taxes varies directly with income. But this does not mean that progression of statutory rates is a necessary feature of progressive taxation. The quite common tendency to define progressive taxation in terms of rate structures, and thus to impart political importance to a technique, is due, it seems to us, to an association to the point of identification of a progressive tax with an income tax;* progression of rates seems to be the very essence of the progressive income tax.

But even if the tax base is income, progression of the statutory rates does not guarantee the progressivity of the tax. It is obviously not progressive if the definition of income as the tax base is "regressive," that is, if a proportional tax imposed on this base would make the distribution of purchasing-power less equal. The political stress on the rate aspect rather than on the base aspect of a progressive income tax is, probably, at least partly responsible for the excessively high top marginal rates in the United Kingdom and the United States and to the regressive erosion of their

---

* Direct taxation as a whole seems to benefit from the halo bestowed by most societies on progressive taxation. Otherwise it would be rather difficult to explain why legislative and executive bodies, almost everywhere, seem to derive satisfaction bordering on pride whenever the proportion of revenue from direct taxes to total revenue rises. For none of the existing definitions of direct and indirect taxes implies that one is superior to the other.

tax bases by the growth of loopholes, escapes, special exemptions, exceptions, preferential treatment, and leakages.[14]

Mixing up progression and progressivity is bad enough, but even worse is the mixing up of progressivity with a "moral" attitude towards taxation in general. The following example is typical of such a confusion.

While the rates of an income tax are fixed by the legislative authorities, rates of indirect taxes are often much more flexible, since the executive body is given some freedom to adjust these rates if it seems wise to do so. This flexibility has great advantages, especially since a legislative change of rates, at best, consumes a lot of time and effort, and since economic outlooks do change frequently. But if our impressions are correct, changes which are made due to changes in the economic outlook are usually legislative, not administrative.

The tax administrator's job, as he sees it, is not to prevent excess effective demand or supply. There are, of course, other officials in the executive branch whose job it is to do just that; but if these latter administrators wish to change the rates of indirect taxes, they too most commonly attempt to achieve their purpose by convincing the legislative body. Tax administrators, on the other hand, might change the rates—if they are allowed to do so—when confronted with personal pressure. Such pressure could possibly come from consumers; but since consumers are usually not organized, and since they are not in any *direct* contact with the administration of *indirect* taxes, they can express their displeasure only in a way that must necessarily influence a legislator more than a tax administrator. Such is not the case, however, when the pressure comes from people in direct contact with the tax administrators, that is, producers and distributors; the tax administrator may often yield to pressure from such sources. Yet as a conscientious official he is in need of a rationalization; he must be sure that he was right when compromising. As a good citizen, who has been reared on the values of his society, he probably believes that taxation should be levied according to ability to pay. He knows very little of the ability to pay of consumers, but as far as producers are concerned, he has balance sheets, statements of profit and loss, cost accounts, and so on—all of which he uses as guidelines. Naturally the first question that enters his mind is: Could this producer absorb an additional tax? Is it *necessary* to lower the tax rate on his commodity? The answers to such questions seem to depend, if not on the producer's total ability to pay, then at least on his income derived from the particular line of production involved. Consequently, a highly profitable firm or industry stands little chance in its endeavors to cut the indirect taxes on the commodities they produce. Administrators of indirect taxes thus unknowingly administer an excess profits tax of their own. Efficient firms and industries are penalized, inefficient ones subsidized. The production of monopolies, which should be expanded to improve the allocation of resources, is curtailed by indirect taxes for the very simple reason that monopolies often have more ability to pay. Risky enterprises are discouraged, for, if successful, they too have a high ability to pay. The price mechanism is severely handicapped in its main job: to redirect resources continuously. And all this is done in very good faith, and in the name of progressive taxation.

The conclusion of this chapter is not that progressive taxation is desirable or undesirable. Our starting point was that it *is* desired, and that this wish for progressive taxation, or for a more equal distribution of income, needs no justification. As we see it, there is a demand for progressive taxation which, like the demand for any commodity or service—granted some consumers' sovereignty exists—must be supplied to some extent. We have also tried to demonstrate, however, that progressive taxation is not a very clear concept. Whether a tax is truly progressive depends on its rate structure, its tax base, the time period considered, the incidence of the tax, the institutional framework of society, the size and nature of government expenditures, other goals to be achieved, and various other factors that we have probably neglected to list. Indeed, it is because of the many factors involved that "consumers" of progressive taxation should take great care to see that what they get is what they asked for.

NOTES

1. Walter J. Blum and Harry Kalven, Jr., *The Uneasy Case for Progressive Taxation* (Chicago: University of Chicago Press, 1953).

2. Henry C. Simons, *Personal Income Taxation* (Chicago: University of Chicago Press, 1938), pp. 18-19.

3. Cf. Dudley Seers, "Has the Distribution of Income Become More Unequal?" *Bulletin of the Oxford University Institute of Statistics,* Vol. 18 (February 1956), pp. 83-84.

4. Allyn A. Young, "Do the Statistics of the Concentration of Wealth in the United States Mean What They Are Commonly Assumed To Mean?" quoted by Mary Jean Bowman in "A Graphical Analysis of Personal Income Distribution in the United States," American Economic Association, *Readings in Income Distribution* (New York: Blakiston Co., 1949), p. 97.

5. Mary J. Bowman, *op. cit.,* p. 97.

6. Cf. J. M. Keynes, *The Economic Consequences of*

the Peace (New York: Harcourt, Brace and Co., 1920), pp. 16-18.

7. See Paul A. Samuelson, in *Federal Tax Policy for Economic Growth and Stability*, Hearings before the Subcommittee on Tax Policy of the Joint Economic Committee (Washington, D.C.: U.S. Government Printing Office, 1956), p. 179.

8. Cf. Musgrave, *The Theory of Public Finance* (New York: McGraw-Hill, 1959), pp. 562-65.

9. That the budget should be discussed as a whole was insisted upon by Antonio de Viti de Marco in his *First Principles of Public Finance* (London: Jonathan Cape, 1936), and more recently by James A. Buchanan, "The Pure Theory of Government Finance," *Journal of Political Economy*, Vol. LVII, (December 1949), pp. 494-505.

10. Cf. M. H. Gopal, *The Theory of Excess Profits Taxation* (Vanvillas Mohalla, Mysore: Bureau of Economic Research, 1947), p. 57.

11. Cf. J. R. Hicks, U. K. Hicks, and C. Rostas, *The Taxation of War Wealth* (Oxford: Clarendon Press, 1941), p. 47.

12. For discussion of the various definitions of progression and of methods of measuring it, see R. A. Musgrave and Thun Thin, "Income Tax Progression, 1929-48," *Journal of Political Economy*, Vol. LVI (December 1948), pp. 498-514. But this highly useful article probably contributed to the confusion of progression with progressivity mainly by the juxtaposition of "Effective Progression"—which is a measure of progressivity—and measures of progression, such as Average Rate Progression and Liability Progression.

13. Cf. Blum and Kalven, *op. cit.*, p. 3 fn.

14. For a discussion of the fiscal significance of the erosion of the individual and corporate income tax base in the United States, see Joseph A. Pechman, "The Individual Income Tax Base," in the 1955 *Proceedings of the National Tax Association* (Sacramento, Calif.: 1956), pp.

304-50. See also *Federal Tax Policy for Economic Growth and Stability*, Hearings before the Subcommittee on Tax Policy of the Joint Economic Committee (Washington, D.C.: U.S. Government Printing Office, 1956), pp. 231-77. For the British experience see, for example, *Royal Commission on the Taxation of Profits and Income, Final Report* (H. M. Stationery office, Cmd. 9474, 1955), pp. 362-63.

CHAPTER FIVE

TAXES AND THE SUPPLY OF RESOURCES

In many countries the subject of taxes has become a channel for much social resentment which is not at all originated only by the payment of taxes. No doubt, some taxes may be extremely harmful—there is no intention here to belittle public finance as an economic subject—but nowhere do they seem to be the determining factors in the development of a country.

For a fully employed economy, taxes of all kinds, like ordinary prices, are but a necessary reflection of a budget restraint. They are intended to release resources from private uses so that they could be transferred to public employment. With full employment, public consumption and/or public investment *necessitates* abstention from equivalent amounts of private consumption or investment. The public-relations problems of the government are created by the nature of much of its expenditures. Since non-taxpayers cannot be excluded from sharing the benefits[1] of many public goods, associations of tax payments with public-goods benefits are greatly weakened. Many may take the benefits for granted, and thus compare two situations where in both they enjoy the same level of public benefits, but where in one case they pay taxes while in the other they do not. Naturally, anyone would find the second case more appealing, but since the real level of government expenditures is the same in both situations, there must be in the second case a tacit assumption that somebody else pays for them, and is necessarily worse off. Tax cheating, like cheating in general, is immoral, and its extent depends mainly on the moral level of the community. But there is nothing irrational about it, at least on the surface. It is for these reasons that the government must minimize the costs of taxes, both economic and psychological, so that their costs in terms of welfare be cut down, and the incentives to evade them be weakened.

The economic effects of taxes are probably not as important as they are usually believed to be.* Truly general taxes have hardly any economic effects of their own; being general they cannot have substitution or re-allocational effects, while their effects on

* Taxes are a very convenient device for illustrating, in courses in price theory, the effects of a change in costs on a single firm or a single industry. Some students never outgrow the mental effects of such exercises, however, not recognizing that partiality is the essence of those "pedagogic" taxes.

real disposable incomes is pre-determined by the level of public expenditures. Having stated this we should hasten to add that truly general taxes do not yet exist in practice. Even a very comprehensive income tax imposing a tax on all incomes that have a rather clear equivalent in money terms will still leave untaxed some flows of utility, like leisure and security, and will not admit as deductible expenses some sources of disutility, like the risk that might have been involved in an eventually successful venture. Even national taxes are only partial from a geographic point of view. And as more or less partial taxes, all taxes have substitution effects—sometimes welcomed, sometimes not —and costs of taxes of the "excess-burden" type are probably underestimated. The literature has dealt mainly with such tax effects on the supply of labor and on the propensities to hoard, to save, and to invest.

EFFECTS ON LABOR SUPPLY

Although labor is the most important single economic resource in any economy, the particular interest in the effects of taxation on its supply is not at all self-explanatory. The rather common condemnation of taxes that seem to curtail the amount of work supplied probably rests on an implicit assumption that the input of labor should be maximized. Yet this very assumption is in direct contradiction to the assumption that work or "effort" is at the margin a source of disutility to its suppliers, an assumption upon which the whole analytical discussion of this problem rests.

The wedge that income taxes impose (at different rates in a nonproportional tax) between the price of labor to its employers and disposable wage payments is, of course, distortive, but so are the employment contracts limiting work hours. As is well known, there has been a secular tendency over the last century or so to curtail both the number of work days per week, and the number of work hours per day. In 1950, the number of work hours per week in the United States was less than half the equivalent number in Europe in 1850.[2] This development, which is commonly approved, is probably a major factor in the very much increased welfare of the economically developed societies. Certainly, in emergencies, the simplest and most reliable way to increase labor supply in man-hours is to increase the standard work week temporarily and with due compensation.

At the same time, in spite of the secular decline in the number of work hours per employed implied by full employment, it has been quite difficult, under normal circumstances, to keep free economies fully employed. As long as nonfrictional unemployment prevails, it is certainly more advantageous to tap the unemployed resources, both human and otherwise, than to manipulate taxes so that labor supply be increased. It makes little sense to complain of the disincentive effects of taxes on that supply when as a matter of fact it is cut again and again with a justified feeling of satisfaction. And, after all, there is no analytical or empirical evidence that taxes do indeed discourage effort.[3] Taxes have both an income effect which—given the assumption that leisure is not an inferior good—provides incentives for more work, and substitution effects which, always working at the margin of decision, provide counterincentives. Ordinarily the ultimate effect depends on the ratio of the marginal tax rate to the average tax rate. The end result of all the inquiries about this question is that progressive taxes either discourage the supply of labor more than proportional (and *a fortiori* regressive) taxes or encourage it less.* This rather agnostic conclusion

* Taxes would have no effect at all on the labor supply of any individual if they corresponded exactly—on the average and in the margin—to the amount of public services provided to that individual; in that case, where no budget redistribution or income takes place, taxes are indeed ordinary prices.

indeed contradicts the intuitive conclusions of many persons that, in a world without taxes, they would have worked more. Yet not only is it very difficult to conceive of such a world but in many cases these introspective conclusions might indeed rest upon comparisons of the actual supply of effort with the irrelevant maximum supply.

Many discussers of the effects of taxation on the supply of labor seem to have in mind labor of a special kind—that is, persons whose income is indeed derived from personal effort, but whose incomes are high enough to be affected by high marginal rates of progressive taxes, and whose supply of work is less institutionally determined, depending as it does, to a greater extent than ordinary labor, on individual decisions. In other words, such discussions refer to executives and to persons included mainly within the sociological category of "professions."

But even in this segment of the population, empirical studies[4] have not demonstrated any significant rise in the incidence of disincentives as a result of high and progressive taxes. Surely patients who are not taken care of by one physician because of tax factors obtain treatment from another, who thus unknowingly "works" more because of taxes! Another reason for the lack of high tax sensitivity among professionals is the extent of nonmonetary advantages which often are a considerable aspect of the compensations of those people. This is not to say, of course, that disincentive effects of steeply progressive taxes on the supply of skilled labor can never be serious. All that is implied is that the general tendency is probably to exaggerate rather than understate such problems.

EFFECTS ON SAVING AND INVESTMENT

Many studies have treated the effects of alternative taxes on the supply of nonpublic savings and to a greater degree their conclusions have depended on the ultimate purpose of the savings, and on the sign and size of the interest elasticity of the supply of savings. Attention to such studies have somewhat subsided, it seems, perhaps because they belong basically to a period in which governments did not conceive of themselves as possible active contributors to the flow of savings. Truly, even today, public sectors in many countries are still negative contributors to this flow, but at least it is widely recognized that governments, even when not ready to undertake investments themselves, can supply a major part of total savings. If they do, and if the tendency in any case is not to let individual citizens determine the rate of savings, a budget surplus would seem a much sharper tool to increase total savings than adjustments in the tax structure.

It is well worth repeating Samuelson's argument on this issue.[5] Since the real savings provided by a budget surplus may be channeled into private investments by means of the monetary system, the idea does not necessarily assume any form of State-Capitalism. Admittedly, the moral basis of a capitalistic system in which entrepreneurship is provided by the "private sector," but resources for new investments are indirectly supplied by the government, is indeed weaker than that of a classical capitalistic system, where individual capitalists not only reap the economic prizes but are truly responsible for running the system. But whether one likes it or not, today's capitalistic society is in most cases a transformed capitalistic society where governments interfere openly in many economic matters, and may legitimately see the level of savings not as a privately determined exogenous variable but as a variable, among the rest, of their own policies.

If the resources are provided by either private or public savings, equivalent investments will surely take place both in the classical "model," where the interest rate shoulders the responsibility for it, and in an economy where major investments are undertaken by the government. In the latter case many common problems including that of the incentive to invest tend to disappear, while many new ones replace them. Government planners are notoriously anxious to invest more than they can; very often more than they should. And since they risk none of their own capital—at worst, they may be fired—they probably tend to optimistically discount heavy capital risks and stress the more favorable possibilities. Losses do occur, of course, so that this over-optimism is distortive from the allocative point of view; but from the incentives point of view there is hardly a problem at all.

But what about economies, like most Western economies, where the investment decision is still made mainly by private entrepreneurs? Taxes do, of course, affect the locations of new investments, not only geographically speaking, but also regarding the choice among industries. Partial taxes of all kinds often result in decreased investments in specific fields. A partial tax signifies an intended discrimination against the industries included in its base, and most investors, not being committed to specific industries, are in a good position to avoid such discrimination. A property tax on houses will somewhat decrease investments in housing, an excise on cars will lower investments in the automobile industry. But all taxes that discriminate against something must also discriminate in favor of something else. Thus although partial taxes may distort the structure of investments, this rather serious consequence does not in itself imply a cut in total investment. As to this latter question, economics does not provide much noncontroversial theories of the investment function even under conditions of certainty of expectations.[6]

There is still disagreement about the ultimate goals of businessmen, and since very little is known about the money equivalents at the margin of "prestige" or of "power" for the multitude of firms, fruitless discussions as to what firms do indeed try to maximize are going to continue. Naturally, without agreement on the very motivations of firms, nothing important can be stated about their investment functions, and an intelligent discussion of the effects of the various taxes on investment is impossible. The sensible way to approach this problem is to assume that firms do try to achieve a specified goal, to shake out the implications of this assumption, and to check whether they are verified by empirical investigations.

Assuming that firms do try to maximize the present value of a stream of money incomes which is expected with certainty, a "universal" income tax will not change the relative profitability of the various investment projects. Indeed, it may very well reduce the amount of disposable savings. But with a given amount of savings, neither the amount nor the structure of investment should be affected by the income tax.

This conclusion follows very clearly in the case of investments out of borrowed funds. Since interest payments on business debts are deductible for income tax purposes, their cost to the paying firms is reduced by the same rate as would be applied to expected profits. With full loss-offsets, any project that seemed attractive *before* the imposition of the tax should remain relatively as attractive *after* the tax is imposed. The same conclusion follows with investments out of equity capital, for again the tax does not change the relative profitability of the various investment possibilities. Under a universal tax and certainty of expectations, it does not matter here whether the income tax is proportional or progressive.

If a tax does not change the relative profitability of

the various investment projects, it does not necessarily leave unchanged the incentives to invest. Naturally, as long as some uses of capital—like hoarding—are not taxed, the incentives to invest may be hampered. The rationale of special tax allowances for new investments is indeed to prevent just such results; their actual effects may actually be *increased* incentives to invest. Take the case of instantaneous depreciation for an asset that is not instantly depreciated in fact. For any firm with taxable incomes born into a world where income tax is taken for granted, there are obvious tax savings whenever it undertakes an investment. With instantaneous depreciation immediately offset against some taxable incomes, the incomes from the new investments are in effect not taxes at all.[7] Under these assumptions, the tax collectors are very fair partners. If t is the tax rate, they contribute immediately t per cent of the cost of the project and will ask for t per cent of the profits. Indeed in many cases investors can, if they wish, restore their pre-tax disposable incomes by multiplying their investment with funds supplied by the new "partners." The tax does not change here the rate of return because it does not apply to new investments; moreover it reduces—by t per cent—either the costs of interest payments or the alternative costs of equity. The investment thus becomes $\frac{l}{l-t}$ more profitable, with the profitability in- increasing with the rate of income tax!

Proportional income tax (with full loss-offsets) and instantaneous depreciation is a unique case of incentive taxation. Here the profitability of new investments is not only restored to its pre-tax level but is increased beyond it. Since the income tax has reduced the rate of return elsewhere, the relative profitability of new investments in depreciable assets is increased to a level higher than the pre-tax one. The incentives to invest should thus be increased absolutely.*

TAXATION AND RISK-TAKING

That the effects of a general proportional income tax on the incentives to invest are not necessarily negative is not at all at odds with the current doctrines on the subject, even when uncertainty of expectations is assumed. This conclusion, however, has not yet gained acceptance outside the rather narrow circle of academic economists. Indeed, the most distinguished studies have invariably concluded that a proportional income tax with full loss-offsets will increase total risk-taking in the economy, and that a progressive income tax with full loss-offsets might have the same results. When no full loss-offsets are allowed, the conclusions remain, basically, that income taxes decrease risk-taking. The same conclusions, incidentally, were reached in models using different definitions of risk—the Domar-Musgrave model defining risk as the probable loss and the Tobin model defining risk as the standard deviation of the outcomes.[8]

* Rolph recognizes that instantaneous depreciation amounts to exempting new investments from income tax, but argues that this restores the incentives to invest to their pre-tax level. See his *The Theory of Fiscal Economics*, *op. cit.*, pp. 278-82. For recent discussions of the devices of incentive taxation, see E. Cary Brown, "Tax Incentives for Investment," *American Economic Review, Papers and Proceedings* (May 1962), pp. 335-45, and "Comments on Tax Credits as Investment Incentives," *National Journal* (June 1962), pp. 198-204; and Sam B. Chase, Jr., "Tax Credits for Investment Spending," *National Tax Journal* (March 1962), pp. 32-52.

For a declining firm, instantaneous depreciation provides an interest-free loan in the same amount. The benefits of the loan are also tax exempt and will increase the total post-tax rate of return. In special cases they may restore it to its pre-tax level, and even beyond.

Needless to say, such conclusions follow from given economic models using certain assumptions and, as usual, one must study the assumptions before applying their conclusions to fiscal policy. Domar and Musgrave, at the end of their study, do review the major limitations on applications of their rather sensational conclusions. One of those limitations, however, seems to us so important that we would tend to accept the conclusions as possible rather than necessary outcomes. This qualification will be discussed here in some length, but the reader should not forget that it is in the nature of a qualification—and not as an objection—to their argument.

Before going into that, however, let us dwell for a moment on the desirability of risk as such. Risk does involve, of course, the possibility of losses. The returns of many capital outlays may be very high, or only moderately so, or zero, or moderately negative, or very highly negative. There is a probability distribution of returns—and it matters not here whether it is determined statistically or subjectively—that has a part which signifies negative returns. Obviously, it would be a spurious risk indeed if these probable losses never materialized; when they do, however, there is a social as well as a private loss.

For the same reasons that it is not at all obvious that more work (= less leisure) should always be encouraged, it is not clear—unless accepted as an axiom—that public policy should be to encourage risk-taking. Granting that some risk-taking is necessary for progress, it still does not follow ineluctably that *more* risk-taking is always for the better. Even when it is widely recognized that more investments are needed to accelerate the rate of economic growth, the necessity of an increase in risk-taking is not a foregone conclusion. For it should be remembered that more risk-taking implies more investment only when it is done at the expense of hoarding, but not at the expense of less risky investments. Gambling, after all, is not usually approved of in most societies, or is considered at best a luxury allowed only for the rich. And it would seem that this attitude does not depend on the ratio of the prices of tickets in a lottery to the actuarial value of the prizes.

It is at least possible that there is some truth in Cannan's conclusion that "the probability is that the classes of investments which on the average return most to the investor are neither the very safest of all nor the very riskiest, but the intermediate classes which do not appeal either to timidity or to the gambling instinct."[9]

Let us return, however, to the main line of argument which assumes that risk-taking is welcomed. In spite of the differences in the very definition of risk, the main new policy-conclusion of the Domar-Musgrave and the Tobin-Hall models is that, owing to a full loss-offset, proportional income taxes have no substitution effect as to the choice between degrees of risks. Let us first follow the Domar-Musgrave model. Their argument runs as follows: A proportional income tax with full loss-offsets cuts risk and returns to the same extent, and therefore has no substitution effect; but since the marginal utility of income is greater at the lower income, "greater risks, *which can be expected to yield greater incomes*, will be taken in order to get income."[10] The underlining is ours, but Paul Streeten here makes quite explicit the assumption that risk-taking, like work, does bring income.

Alternatively, the argument may be stated in terms of utilities. The proportional income tax plus loss-offsets cuts losses and gains to the same extent, but because of diminishing marginal utility of income, a tax at a rate t absorbs less than the tth part of the utility of the gain, while the loss-offset offsets more than the tth part of the utility of loss. For this very reason, any risky investment that was considered profitable before the imposition of the income tax will be even more so with the income tax plus offsets.

The argument thus depends on the assumption of diminishing marginal utility of income; yet there are good reasons to doubt whether the marginal utility of income is indeed constantly decreasing. As a rationalization for the coexistence of insurance and gambling, Friedman and Savage[11] suggest a utility function with a segment convex from above (that is, decreasing marginal utility), followed by a segment concave from above (that is, increasing marginal utility), possibly followed by another concave section. Markowitz, on the other hand, suggests[12]—and his suggestion also rationalizes both insurance and gambling and is supported by "introspective empiricism"—that the utility function has three inflection points, with the middle point at the customary level of wealth, where the marginal utility of income is increasing. In both cases the Domar-Musgrave conclusions may be reversed.* Moreover, the application of the assumption of diminishing marginal utility of income to corporations also raises many additional thorny problems.

Although the dependence of the analysis on the assumption of diminishing marginal utility of income is basic, it does have the advantage of being clear. Such is not the case with one of the assumptions explicitly mentioned by Domar and Musgrave†—that

* The Markowitz hypothesis is especially important here, since taxation does affect the customary level of wealth. Therefore, increasing marginal utility of income for additions to that level (and decreasing marginal utility of income for substractions from that level) should follow as part of the hypothesis itself rather than accidentally, as in the Friedman-Savage case.

† It would be worthwhile to quote the authors' statement on this point in full. "Throughout our discussion the investor's

is, that the tax does not change the investor's wealth. On the face of it, this assumption might seem innocent, but in many cases it is inconsistent with the main body of economic theory.

For, if the tax is imposed on incomes from all sources including wages and salaries, incomes from "bonds" (which will stand here for unearned incomes which are relatively riskless), as well as incomes from "equities" where risk is much greater, it *necessarily* reduces the investors' flow of disposable incomes and their present values—that is, their wealth. As post-tax poorer men, they have to make their investment decisions again. The tax (with the loss-offsets) did not change the returns for risks, but increased the utility of gain, and also the disutility of loss. Under the circumstances, some persons might be more willing to take a risk, in the hope of increasing incomes, while others might be less willing, being afraid to lose what they have. It is at least possible that although utility derived from the probable gain of an investment exceeded the disutility of the probable loss before the imposition of the tax—and therefore the investment was undertaken (and would have been taken *a fortiori* after the tax had it not affected disposable incomes or values of investments)—that the tax still so increases the utility of money (as income or asset) that from the new position where decisions have to take place that very investment is rejected as unprofitable.

It does not matter here whether the income tax

_____

wealth was assumed to be constant. Now it is likely that as the result of the tax the investor's wealth will change, which in turn may change his indifference pattern. That is, his general attitude towards risk-taking may become more or less favorable. This secondary adjustment has not been taken into account, since the analysis is limited to the immediate effects of the tax on the investor's decision. The effect of taxation on wealth is in itself a complex problem, particularly because the effects of alternative taxes and/or expenditures must be taken into consideration" (Domar and Musgrave, *op. cit.*, p. 523).

applies to all incomes, or to all unearned incomes, or only to profits—that is, a partial tax on "equities," the specially risky investments, explicitly exempting "income from bonds." In the latter case, capitalization of the tax seems quite obvious. The owners of "equities" realize capital losses, which might negatively affect readiness for further risk-taking, and, to repeat, as poorer persons, they may be either less or more willing to take risk. Inconclusiveness is obviously going to prevail here unless explicit assumptions are made about the income-utility function.* All that is proved is that with proportional income taxes and full loss-offsets a given individual with a given disposable income will take more risk than he would if he had the same disposable income but no tax to pay.

Basically, assuming no special aversion or liking towards risk, entrepreneurial decisions depend on weighing the utility from gain against the disutility from loss. And the results of such weighing do not depend only on market opportunities, as the following case will illustrate. Say that an individual is faced with a choice between investing a given amount of money in either project A or B. To make things simpler, suppose that in A there are 60 per cent chances of a gain of $50,000, and 40 per cent chances of a loss of $20,000. In B the chances are 99 per cent of a gain of $10,000, and 1 per cent of a loss of $100. Assuming a logarithmic utility function,† the same individual will much prefer A if his disposable income is $60,000 but will reject A in favor of B, if it is

---

* True, it is always possible for investors to reshuffle their portfolios, and it is legitimate to start the analysis from a position where they have only cash; but the amount of cash will also be affected by the tax.

† This is not a very high elasticity. If equal burden is to be imposed on all taxpayers, arguments for progressive taxation must assume a quicker rate of decline of marginal utility.

$30,000. For in the latter case, the marginal utility of the last dollar lost under an unsuccessful A is eight times higher than the marginal utility of the last dollar of gain under a successful A. Under the circumstances, an income tax at a proportional rate of 50 per cent that halves disposable income to $30,000 certainly does not increase risk-taking. All we can say is that *if*, in spite of the decline in disposable income, a given project or portfolio is still the most attractive, then proportional taxation plus loss-offsets will indeed increase risk-taking. But that is a big *if*, indeed.

It should be made clear that our argument, if valid, does not detract from the great desirability of full loss-offsets, neither from an inquiry point of view nor as an incentive device when more investments are needed.

Moreover, the qualification does not apply to a differential analysis of the effects of an income tax on risk-taking. If the income tax substitutes another tax with an equal burden on investors, the Domar-Musgrave conclusion does indeed follow. For in this common case the investors' wealth may indeed be taken as given.

There are also specific cases where the by-now orthodox conclusions hold without any qualifications. The presence of a proportional income tax plus full loss-offsets in any country should make risk-taking in that country more appealing to prospective foreign investors. In this case there is indeed no effect on either the size of the investors' disposable incomes in other countries or on the values of their portfolios. A similar case, not involving foreign investments, is where the tax and loss-offset apply to new investments only.

Another case is that of a quasi-benefit income tax, the proceeds of which are used by the government to provide services to investors which they previously bought in the market. Here again there should be no (or almost no) change in real disposable incomes. In other words, the differential effect of a proportional income tax with full loss-offsets is to increase risk-taking. It may—and may not—also be its absolute effect.

The same conclusion follows with Tobin's definition of risks as the dispersion of outcomes. Our only qualification to that analysis is that the income and wealth effects of the tax may change not only the opportunity line between yield and dispersion but also the indifference curve between the two.

Naturally the space allotted here to this qualification may distort its importance even in our own eyes. The main point is indeed the one stressed by Domar-Musgrave and Tobin-Hall. And while some academic economists may overstate it, is still has a long way to go before it will get its rightful recognition from those responsible for fiscal policy.

CONCLUSIONS

It is evident that the effects of general taxes on the supply of resources are not usually serious. As long as taxes do not change relative prices, they cause no distortions in the allocation of resources and their supply. By exempting the utility of leisure or by disregarding the disutility of risk, taxes do become somewhat discriminating, but the inconclusiveness which has been typical of so much of this chapter implies that the effects of general taxes imposed on money incomes only are also not severe.* Income from all sources—as long as it is from all sources—has many of the economic features of rent, and the Henry Georgian idea of a tax on economic surplus may be re-

---

* With mobility of either labor or capital to other political units, a general income tax imposed by one jurisdiction may be very partial in practice.

interpreted to mean a nondiscriminating tax on income. Taxes are probably much costlier in their "excise-tax effects"* on the efficiency of the use of existing resources than in their effects on the amount of those resources at a given point of time.

NOTES

1. The influence of Musgrave's treatise *The Theory of Public Finance* is probably too obvious to even be mentioned. See Paul A. Samuelson, "Diagrammatic Exposition of a Theory of Public Expenditure," *Review of Economics and Statistics*, Vol. XXXVII (November 1955), pp. 350-56; and Paul B. Trescott, "The Burdens of Government Finance," *Public Finance*, Vol. XI, No. 2 (1956) pp. 164-76.

2. Cf. W. S. Woytinski and E. S. Woytinski, *World Population and Production* (New York: The Twentieth Century Fund, 1953), pp. 366-67.

3. See R. Musgrave, *The Theory of Public Finance* (New York: McGraw-Hill, 1959), Chap. 11; and George F. Break, "Income Taxes Wage Rates and the Incentives to Supply Labor Services," *National Tax Journal*, Vol. VI, No. 4 (December 1953), pp. 333-52, and the bibliography in his fn. 6 and 9.

4. See, for example, G. F. Break, "Income Taxes and Incentives to Work: An Empirical Study," *American Eco-*

---

* The term is Arnold C. Harberger's. In his important study, "The Corporation Income Tax: An Empirical Appraisal," he measures the excise-tax costs of the U.S. corporation income tax and concludes that this tax introduces distortions costing the U.S. economy between $1 and $1.5 billion per year. See *Tax Revision Compendium*, Vol. I (Washington, D.C.: U.S. Government Printing Office, 1959), pp. 231-50.

nomic Review, Vol. XLVII (September 1957), pp. 529-49.

5. See Chapter 4, p. 27.

6. For a survey of modern theories of investment, see John R. Meyer and Edwin Kuh, *The Investment Decision* (Cambridge, Massachusetts: Harvard University Press, 1957), Chap. 2. A later important contribution is Yehuda Grunfeld, "The Determinants of Corporate Investment," in *The Demand for Durable Goods,* ed. by A. C. Harberger (Chicago: University of Chicago Press, 1960), pp. 211-66.

7. Cf. E. Cary Brown, "Business-Income Taxation and Investment Incentives," *Income Employment and Public Policy, Essays in Honor of Alvin H. Hansen* (New York: W. W. Norton, 1948), pp. 300-16, reprinted in American Economic Association *Readings in the Economics of Taxation* (Homewood, Illinois: 1959), pp. 525-37; and Earl R. Rolph, *The Theory of Fiscal Economics* (Berkeley: University of California Press, 1954), Chaps. 11, 12.

8. See Evsey D. Domar and Richard A. Musgrave, "Proportional Income Taxation and Risk-Taking," reprinted in American Economic Association, *Readings in the Economics of Taxation, op. cit.,* pp. 493-524; James Tobin, "Liquidity Preference as Behavior Towards Risk," *The Review of Economic Studies,* No. 67 (February 1958), pp. 65-86; Challis A. Hall, Jr., *Fiscal Policy for Stable Growth* (New York: Holt-Rinehart, 1960), esp. Chaps. II, VI, VII. In Chap. 14 of his *The Theory of Public Finance* (New York: McGraw-Hill, 1959), Musgrave rediscusses the issue, and his footnotes 1 on pp. 313 and 316, respectively, mention other leading contributions.

9. The quotation from Edwin Cannan's article on "Profit," in *Dictionary of Political Economy,* ed. by H. H. Inglis Palgrave, is cited in Friedman and Savage, "The Utility Analysis of Choices involving Risk," in American Economic Association *Readings in Price Theory,* selected by George J. Stigler and Kenneth E. Boulding (Homewood, Illinois, 1952), p. 65.

10. Quoted from Paul Streeten, "The Effect of Taxation on Risk-Taking," *Oxford Economic Papers*, Vol. 5 (October 1953), p. 272.

11. Cf. Friedman and Savage, *op. cit.*, pp. 80-86.

12. Harry Markowitz, "The Utility of Wealth," *Journal of Political Economy*, Vol. IX (April 1952), pp. 151-58.

CHAPTER SIX

ON INDIRECTNESS
IN TAXATION

It is often argued that outlay taxes do not discourage
the supply of some factors of production as much as
do income taxes.* Such arguments may depend on
differences experienced in practice between the distributional effects of existing taxes belonging to the
two categories. They may also depend on the assumption that outlay taxes, unlike income taxes, do not
change the relative prices of consumption at the
present or at the future, and thus do not affect the
incentives to save. And indeed this is a valid argument
if outlay taxes are exclusively consumption taxes, if

* Some of the problems discussed here are more relevant to
countries where the role of partial taxes is greater, the nominal
rate of interest higher, and a stable external value politically
less important.

no changes in the rates of consumption taxes are expected, and if all savings are intended to be dissaved in the future. When these conditions are fulfilled, income taxes will, and outlay taxes will not, weaken the incentives to save, if (again!) saving is indeed positively related to the rate of interest.

Yet, intuitively, it seems to us that the comparative advantage often ascribed to outlay taxes is basically a psychological one that does not depend logically on the economic theory of consumers' behavior. If this is so, and if the very ascription is valid to begin with, it is important to find out just what are the sources of that psychological advantage.

As Ursula Hicks has indicated,[1] the direct-indirect classification was clearly in origin, and is still essentially, an administrative distinction, with the direct taxes being those which are either directly assessed or directly collected. The administrative and legislative *intention* in the case of indirect taxes is that the set of people who pay the tax to the tax collectors would be recompensed by another set, usually much greater in number, the intended taxpayers. Since no-shifting usually means absorption of taxes by profits-receivers, forward or backward shifting of parts of indirect taxes must have been taken for granted whenever the tax rates exceeded the rate of profits. But in the case of partial taxes, like excises, backward shifting to lenders is hardly apt to take place, and although backward shifting to labor cannot be ruled out, it is almost inevitable that prices of the final goods will rise when downward money-wage rigidity is assumed. This result, Professor Shoup argues,[2] is the one intended by legislators and administrators and which under normal circumstances they prefer. For even when their intentions are not truly materialized, such a rise may give the impression that they have been.

It is taken for granted here that to use ultimate

incidence as the criterion in distinguishing, *ex-post*, between indirect taxes and direct taxes would require in each case elaborate econometric studies, but that does not make the legislative intentions completely irrelevant for other purposes. Even for purposes of empirical studies of distribution of tax burdens, it is of some importance to estimate also the distribution of these burdens as intended by the legislative bodies. Likewise, the statement that commodities cannot pay taxes themselves is self-evident but does not deprive the distinction of all relevance in other contexts between taxes imposed *directly* on households and taxes imposed on households through increases in prices of commodities. Truly, if human behavior were illusionlessly rational, such "intermediate" tax targets would be of no importance. But humans being human, many of them do tend to think of indirect taxes as taxes "on commodities."

Many of the alleged and actual advantages of indirect taxes depend on their being counted as elements in the prices paid for the purchase of goods and services. Since the payment of even a rather general sales tax depends on a speciously volitional act of purchase, there is always the feeling that the tax is not really unavoidable. And since market prices are sometimes rather arbitrary indeed and may be often considered by the public to be even more so than they actually are, there may be only a slight difference between the resentment of having to pay for the purchased goods themselves and that of having to pay for the taxes imposed on them. Indeed, consumers often seem to have implicitly accepted taxes on commodities as reflecting, as if in accordance with the Benefit Principle, the payments for government contributions towards the production of the purchased goods. Depending on the nature of the tax, and the level(s) where it is imposed, purchasers often do not know at all how much tax is included in the price.[3] Instead of receipts, taxpayers bring home cartons of cigarettes, bottles of whiskey, or new cars. They are not too dissimilar from the natives in pre-union Natal who, when given the choice between a marriage fee and a hut tax, expressed their preference for the former on the ground that "when a man marries his heart is glad, everything looks pleasant to him and he is in humor to pay whatever is asked of him."[4] Certainly, this psychological feature does play some role in easing the payment of almost every tax on commodities. Yet there are other pain-relieving features which are also operative—among which is the fact that the tax is paid in small doses and there is no direct confrontation between the taxpayer and the tax collector, which, it must be admitted, is tormenting to most taxpayers.

Whether or not these psychological advantages of taxes on commodities are indeed economic advantages depends on one's general outlook. If the philosophy of consumers' sovereignty is adhered to, the marginal utility of government services to the community as a whole should be equal to the community's marginal disutility of paying taxes, and in order to achieve this, taxpayers should be made conscious of the costs involved. The position taken here, however, is that at a given moment of time this should apply only to budget considerations which are actually at the margin of decision; total psychological costs, like all others, should be minimized. When it is generally recognized that the level of government expenditures is sub-optimal, there are good reasons to try to understate the costs of finance even at the margin.

Even if taxes on commodities did not raise prices, but instead reduced factors incomes, many people as taxpayers would have preferred them, *ceteris paribus*, to income taxes. Indeed, in the context of income taxes, many people prefer that the tax be withheld at the source, in spite of the loss of potential interest incomes. Objections to withholding are commonly voiced by groups for whom it is easier to at least partially evade the taxes under alternative methods of collection. The common man, it is submitted here, prefers withholding, because he is worried lest otherwise he would not have the money needed when the tax payments are due, because he hates to see his liquid balances go down considerably when tax payments become due without acquiring offsetting assets, and mainly because withholding allows him to worry less about taxes and spares him the frustration of having to pay taxes allegedly willingly.

True, most taxpayers have only a vague idea (and their spouses even less) of how much is withheld from them. Yet receipts are perennial witnesses and he who wishes to know can always find out. "Taxes on commodities" have the additional advantage that, whatever their incidence, the taxpayer really does not know how much he pays. To answer such a question he would have to know the quantities of taxed goods he consumes; what are the taxes imposed, directly or indirectly, on their production at all its stages; to what extent these taxes are reflected in relative increases in prices of the taxed goods, and corresponding relative decreases in other prices; and to what extent falls in factors income, including his own, take place. If absolute decreases in factors money incomes (excluding profits) are ruled out, indirect taxes will in many cases necessarily increase the price level. This tax-induced price rise, upheld by monetary conditions, does not, as we know, settle the issue of incidence—that issue depends on further developments—but it may impart to indirect taxes some additional psychological advantages.

Money illusion, where it does exist, usually implies a preference to have unavoidable cuts in real incomes

—that is, money incomes deflated by the price level—
by way of increases in price level, rather than by way
of decreases in money incomes. The existence of
money illusion cannot be easily proved, however.
Asking people whether they prefer their income to
change through changes in disposable money incomes
or through changes in the price level probably misses
a major part of the point at issue. People might be
money-illusioned simply because they are unaware
that these very changes are taking place, or because
the change is not very big and is simply one of many
other changes that is occurring at the same time. This
is not to say, of course, that money illusion is not a
bubble that could easily burst.

In some cases, the phenomenon described as money
illusion may reflect simple utility maximization. Any
individual who is a net borrower and whose commit-
ments are fixed in money terms will indeed prefer
that his taxes be in the form of an increase in the price
level; that will at least somewhat relieve his burden
as a borrower. Wage and salary earners may prefer
to have cuts in real incomes through a rise in the
costs of living, hoping to be at least partly compensated for the cuts either automatically or by means
of collective bargaining; decreases in money incomes
may seem to be much more *final* than a rise in prices.

Still there are some indications pointing to the
existence of a "true" money illusion. That money
wages, but not real wages, may be rigid downwards
has become a very common assumption in economic
theory, at least since Keynes, and this assumption—
reflecting beliefs about reality—surely signifies money
illusion on the part of labor.[5] The rather weak correlation found between rates of interest and the rates
of price changes may also be partly explained by
money illusions.[6] Also, capital levies on money balances—which when replacing equivalent amounts of

deficit financing do not impose much of a real burden on those holding these assets at the beginning of the "period"—often stir much stronger objections than devaluations of the external value of currencies which, with monetary support, may impose much greater burdens on those who happen to hold obligations. Similarly, many people fail to realize that imputed incomes, like imputed rents and interest, are incomes that affect their welfare (and ability to pay taxes), like incomes received in money terms, and indeed in the U.S.A. and many other countries such incomes are not subject to income tax. Likewise, many people believe commercial radio or television to be costless, at least to them, since they are supported by "sponsors." The two last cases illustrate a somewhat different kind of "money illusion," but even here the essence of the phenomenon is that there is greater sensitivity to money incomes than to real incomes.

This greater sensitivity to changes in money incomes, as compared to changes in the purchasing-power of those incomes, may be due to important socio-psychological factors.

Income in Western economies, and elsewhere, is the most important single stratifying factor. For an independent earner or enterprise, increased incomes are the undisputed indicators of success; for the employed a sign of approval. Indeed, the whole system of aspirations might have been formulated in terms of money incomes; consequently, reductions in such income cannot help having repercussions in noneconomic spheres.[7] If the price level rises there will obviously be some adjustments in the money scale of aspirations, but sometimes there is a considerable lag. Often, the information about the change in the price level is not fully transmitted to the breadwinner. The purchaser in the market notices that more money income is needed if the same real level of purchases is to be maintained, but for the spender—very often the wife of the income-earner—a rise in prices has only an income effect: more money is needed. Depending on the tempers of the household members and on objective possibilities, there may or may not be an increase in the supply of factors of production under the control of the household; a decrease in that supply is certainly not expected. On the other hand, when a tax is directly imposed on money income, the income-earner not only receives less disposable income, but often feels frustrated and vexed. He may resent the intrusion of the government between himself and his employer much more than he does the wedges of indirect taxes somewhere in the price structure.

Anthony Downs has made some interesting suggestions that may provide still another rationale for money illusions in the fiscal area.[8] According to Downs, men are more apt to exert political pressure and influence in their roles as income-receivers than in their roles as income-spenders.[9] Since their revenues come from fewer public-policy areas than do their consumers' outlays, their attention is naturally directed to matters that might affect them mainly as income-receivers. In this regard, Downs stresses the important points that the exertion of political pressure is not costless, and that attaining information which is necessary for the exertion of any influence has its own price in terms of time and mental energy. The information as to policy matters that might affect an individual as a producer is both quantitatively more important to him and also easier and cheaper to get than information regarding industries to which his only relation is that part of his income, and it is usually a small part, expended on their products. It is also simpler to judge the significance and the reliability of information about an industry where one is employed. People are thus naturally more alert to changes in money incomes than to changes in other prices that affect their real incomes.

For the same reasons, labor unions are not to be expected to act for their members' interests as consumers with the same aggressive spirit characteristic of their efforts for their members' interests as producers. Labor union leaders, like all officials, have their motivations and expectational compensations and rewards, and like all politicians they are usually interested in re-nomination, re-election, and promotion. They feel that in the eyes of union members they are responsible, at least to some extent, for their members' money wages, but definitely not for the price level, which seems to members to be an unrelated matter. Under such circumstances it is only logical that union leaders will always ask for higher money wages as long as there are no sanctions from a non-sympathetic government or pressures from a sympathetic one which organized labor supports.

The relative weakness of consumer pressure groups may also be ascribed to factors perhaps more fundamental than the relative "unprofitability" of investing time and energy to influence policy in spheres which affect individuals only as consumers of some specific commodities. Although income-receivers and income-spenders are obviously the same persons, income is received and spent in two different social situations. In a modern capitalistic society, the production process, which is the source of the income received, is characterized, to a much greater extent than the consumption sphere, by the properties of an economic action.

The purely economic action, to use terms introduced by Parsons,[10] is (a) *universalistic*—that is, it reflects a disposition on the part of the actor in a given situation to respond towards other people in conformity with general standards rather than in the light of their possession of properties—like kinship—which have a particular relation to the actor's own properties (opposite—*particularistic*); it is (b) *specific*—that is, concerned with one rather than a whole range of possible spheres of contact (opposite—*diffuse*); and lastly, it is (c) *oriented toward achievement* rather than ascription, so that specific performances are preferred to attributes that are essentially independent of past, present, or prospective performances.

But while the main purpose of production is to provide goods and services for consumption, people as consumers are primarily family-men, and their actions in the social situations where consumption actually occurs are rather particularistic, diffuse, and oriented towards ascription rather than achievement. The dominant properties of the social situation affect the attitudes of the individuals involved so that, we would venture to suggest, income-receivers as producers are intrinsically more "organizable" than consumers who as family-men automatically belong to a primary group and a most conservative one. The particularistic, diffuse, and ascriptive relations of the family naturally tint the political outlook of consumers towards conservatism.

An organization of consumers is unlikely to succeed therefore for various reasons; being organized initially in family groups, they have no urge to form an organization. Moreover, consumer organizations conceptually should include "everybody and his brother," that is, should be as wide as society itself and therefore both functionless and unfunctioning. But as Katona indicates,[11] the whole situation does not and cannot encompass everything; the whole to be grasped as a whole must have closures. Thus, to be fiscally influential, pressure groups *must* exclude at least some sectors in the economy; everybody cannot be protected from everybody. It is for just such reasons that consumers' organizations are apt to center around some *specific* products—hence, organizations of pipe-smokers and scooter-riders—and recreational purposes come to dominate it. The chances of its turning into a fighting organization which exerts effective pressure are extremely slim.

Income-receivers, on the other hand, do need organizations, for both practical and emotional reasons. Thus some organizations exist primarily to supply their members with a feeling of "belonging." On the practical side, producer organizations often tend to view each other as means to ends rather than as whole personalities, and for this reason are apt to be aggressively dynamic.

The differences between attitudes of accidental members of a group who are pretty much born into it and hardly notice it, and attitudes of members of groups that are limited and where belonging depends on volitional activities, are undoubtedly considerable. Naturally, "group coherence and group centered motivational forces are usually most pronounced in groups composed of interacting members who are united in face to face situations."[12] But even when personal meetings of members are rare, members may be quite conscious of the differences between those who "belong" and those who do not.

In areas other than taxation, similar factors might have been responsible for continuous wage-price spirals long after the time it should have been made clear to both "labor" and "capital" that the race was not helping them any. Since rising wages constitute an achievement for a producing actor for whom economic achievements are of major importance (since in the economic sphere they are the *ends)*, while rising commodity prices are a loss for a consuming actor for whom the whole economic sphere is but means to other ends and therefore of much less importance, the gains of rising money incomes are not, in the psychological field, completely offset by the losses of rising prices. Indeed, in a capitalistic society, inflation seems to be a temporarily effective method of "mollifying class conflict," a "social lubricant" that permits one pressure group to increase its money income without decreasing that of anyone else, and therefore without arousing the volume and vehemence of opposition which might be expected otherwise.[13] Inflation allows conflicting social groups the illusion of being in the harmonious position where each group is ready to grant the demands of the other, provided it gets its own demands approved.

Not only are consumers groups weaker than producers groups, but, in any case, governments themselves tend to pay much more attention to pressure exerted upon them by the latter. This tendency may reflect puritan attitudes, mistaking means for ends and thus eyeing consumption as wasteful, and it may also be a result of the reliance of political parties on economic support of groups with particular interests in the field of production and distribution. In some instances, the readiness of governments to pay a price for peaceful relations with producing groups may reflect a political dependence of a deeper nature. As already noted, the government in many contemporary economies has accepted the responsibility of securing full employment for the labor force; yet in a basically free enterprise economy, the government cannot fulfill this pledge without the very active participation of the necessary partners—private business firms and labor organizations.

Similarly, if a government tries to control transactions involving foreign exchange, and to fix or regulate the rate of the foreign exchange, it immediately needs the cooperation of exporters, importers, bankers, all of whom are members of private economic organizations. In effect, the very intention of modern government to play a growing part in economic activities makes them in many ways more dependent on producers groups, and very rarely on consumers. Even the legislative body may have a much more sensitive ear to producer demands.

To return to the area of taxation, the relative weakness of consumers' consciousness of their own interests may be illustrated by the "natural" preference of most citizens to rely as far as possible on tariffs as a source of fiscal revenue. Most economists, however, are not easily impressed by the strength of grass-roots protectionist sentiments. Indeed, the very process of economic education often starts with discussions of "comparative advantage" as applied to international trade. Those who are convinced may even be oversold on the idea and mistakenly conclude that tariffs are the worst of all partial taxes. But not everyone will be so convinced, and more importantly, the very need to argue back and forth implies that, to begin with, there is a rather strong opposition to the free trade argument. Certainly we hear no consumers' outcry against tariffs; indeed, they know much less about prices in other countries than they do about prices in their own. Some may know that local prices of foreign products depend also on the exchange rate which, in a flexible exchange rate system, changes often in any case, and in a rigid exchange rate system depends to some extent on the level of duties on imports and exports. So, as taxes, tariffs are indeed somewhat vague, and they also vex a comparatively small number of persons. Not counting consumers, the only nonforeigners who are obviously burdened by tariffs are importers, who, in many countries, are wrongly considered to be easily replaceable, and who only rarely wield much political influence. Even when it is not assumed that tariffs are partly shifted to foreign suppliers, they are considered in some emotional sense to be taxes on "foreigners."

"Foreigners," incidentally, are not necessarily citizens of another country. In some places in the Near East, and possibly elsewhere, taxes like the *octroi*,* not basically different from tariffs, are still imposed by rather autonomous authorities of units smaller than the state. This usually happens when the main reliance and sense of belonging of the population is toward those smaller units.

THE CASE FOR INDIRECT INCOME TAXES†

If the economic costs of general taxes, whether on income or on outlay, are not very important, two conclusions seem to follow. The first and more important is that, unless nonneutral effects are clearly intended, taxes should be imposed in such a way as to affect choices as little as possible. The general rule that the elasticity of demand for (and the supply elasticity of) a subgroup of commodities or of factors of production is higher than the demand elasticity for (and the supply elasticity of) the group as a whole is very useful in this respect. Special tax treatments which may look most innocuous can be quite harmful in the long run. The common opinion that actual taxes do inflict a burden on the economy distinct from the necessary reduction in private expenditures thus does not necessarily contradict the exemption of general taxes—in a practical sense—from much guilt.

But it is also quite plausible that the high costs

* The octroi is a local tax levied on certain articles, such as foodstuffs, on their admission into a city.

† The proportional and comprehensive value-added tax suggested here is similar in some respects to the now famous French *taxe sur la valeur ajoutée*, which, so it seems, will be the main indirect tax of the European Common Market. Unfortunately this book went to press before the publication of several relevant studies, including *The Role of Direct and Indirect Taxes in the Federal Revenue System* (Princeton: Princeton University Press, 1964) and the *Report of the Committee on Turnover Taxation* (London: His Majesty's Stationery Office, CMND 2300, 1964).

often ascribed to taxation are mainly psychological—
a fact that should not make them less important, nor
even less important for the economy as such. Economists usually do not deal with them only because the
tools of economic analysis are inadequate for the purpose. Yet the psychological disadvantages of taxes
should not be underestimated, as indeed they are not
by both tax legislators and administrators. The development of researches in fiscal psychology[14] which has
taken place in Italy,[15] Germany, and elsewhere on the
Continent is therefore to be welcomed by economists,
even if their own contributions as economists to such
investigations must be amateurish.

At the same time, economists should realize that
their own recommendations may quite often be rejected by the fiscal psychologist, just as they are by
the politician himself. Worse still, the psychologist
might submit scientific counterarguments against the
economist's conclusions. And what should legislators
do with the economist's recommendation against, say,
excises if it happened to contradict that of the fiscal
psychologist to which, most understandably, the legislators are more sensitive? Truly, conflicts among various considerations may be expected to arise often in
the field of taxation as elsewhere, and it is the necessity of choice which makes decision-making difficult
and important. Yet, at the same time, it is desirable
to limit conflicts to real and thus unavoidable areas
of disagreement. Some conflicts are surely artificial in
the sense that a better understanding of the problems
would have shown that the allegedly conflicting goals
were not mutually exclusive.

In this sense, the conflict between the psychological
advantages of indirect taxes and the distributional
and allocational advantages of a general income tax
is false to the extent that it does not depend on differences in the generality of the two categories of taxes.

It would be a great pity indeed if a preference for indirect taxation, which the fiscal psychologist is almost certain to sustain, were to prevail upon distributional value judgments and rational preferences for more efficient allocation of resources, and result in the adoption of distortive and regressive indirect taxes. For, it is submitted here, the quality of indirectedness may also be imparted to general income taxes.

If there is a social agreement that either public consumption or public investment is below their optimal level and should therefore be increased at the cost of private uses of resources, and if it is believed that indirect taxes are less costly from the psychological viewpoint, the tendency to endorse even regressive indirect taxes on commodities would seem to be almost obvious, especially when the increase in government expenditures is considered to be both urgent and progressive from a distributional point of view. Thus it is easy to understand why Galbraith, the main protagonist of this argument is quite ready to allow sales taxes to increase their fiscal role considerably[16] so that taxes on private consumption will pay for the increased public consumption. But why a sales tax if an income tax can be made indirect without losing its essence?

If all income taxes were withheld at the source, much of the sense of indirectedness would have already been imparted to them, and that clearly could be easily done, at least with proportional income taxes. If such taxes were not only collected through the firms which are the sources of the taxable incomes but were also legally imposed on such firms, it would indeed be difficult—at least in a closed economy—to tell the difference between indirect outlay taxes and indirect income taxes, as long as both were general. With the new income taxes being general they should cause no more change in the allocation of resources

than do ordinary income taxes. And since they would
be imposed on firms, their chances of increasing the
price level would be no less than those of ordinary
outlay taxes. Suppose that all firms, including all public employers, were to pay a tax at the rate of, say,
25 per cent on payments of wages, salaries, rent, interest, and on the remaining profits, whether dis-
tributed or not. Such a tax might be viewed as a
combination of pay-roll taxes and taxes on "unearned
incomes." But the very combination would deprive
these taxes of the properties usually ascribed to them.
Alternatively, it might be viewed as a value-added tax;
its indirectness being clear in both cases. But the
technical point—that the tax is legally imposed on
firms—should not mislead us: it is still a tax on all
incomes, and as such does not differ in its effects from
a simple income tax.

The relatively new idea of a value-added tax has
been developed as a rather ingenious solution to the
problems of the level at which sales taxes should be
imposed. As a multiple-stage sales tax which imposes
at each level only a part of the total tax, the value-
added tax thus reduces somewhat the incentives to
cheat the fiscus, while at the same time, it does not
encourage vertical integration of firms. But surely a
value-added tax is also an income tax deducted at the
source—an indirect income tax, if you wish.

Following Musgrave,[17] let us remember that in an
all-consumption economy 1) it is a matter of indifference whether a general tax on transactions is assessed
on the seller's or on the buyer's side of the market;
2) it is a matter of indifference whether a general tax
is assessed on the product or on the factor transactions
of any particular transactor; and, as a result of that,
3) there is an equivalence between a personal income
tax and a general sales tax. A general income tax is
a tax imposed on the seller's side of the market, that

is, on those selling economic services,* while the value-added tax is one imposed on buying those services, so that the first proposition establishes the equivalence of these two taxes which, incidentally, is not limited to an all-consumption model.† A value-added tax remains a tax on all incomes even when savings (and capital formation) are introduced.[18]

The value-added tax, as an indirect income tax, could be imposed on all incomes derived during the tax period from the supply of all economic resources, that is, on national income. As such, unlike the French "Taxe sur la valeur ajoutée" and the Michigan "Business Receipts Tax," it should exclude depreciation as a matter of course,‡ and cannot include capital gains of any kind.

In an open economy, that is, everywhere, the value-added tax should be accompanied by a tax with the same rate on all imports, so that imports will not be artificially encouraged. The value-added and the import taxes together constitute a uniform tax on all resources available. The discussion that follows assumes that such an import tax is imposed.

---

* In practice, income taxes may be also imposed on receipts which contribute to the ability to pay, though they are not payments for economic services.

† By equivalence we do not mean complete identity of economic effects; Musgrave himself lists several reasons that could bring about differences between the economic effects of the two taxes (see *The Theory of Public Finance, op. cit.,* pp. 361-62). As a matter of fact, the very idea of substituting one for the other would make no sense were the equivalence complete.

‡ Shoup distinguishes between a consumption type value-added tax, where depreciation is deducted, and an income type, where the cost of all capital equipment bought from other firms is subtracted. The two are equal for the economy as a whole when the economy is "stabilized," that is, where there is no net capital formation. Cf. Shoup, "Theory and Background of the Value-Added Tax," 1955 Proceedings of the 48th Conference of the National Tax Association, pp. 9-13.

Since a general value-added tax is equivalent to a general income tax, it is, as Shoup pointed out,[19] as neutral as the latter tax. It is especially important to note that the common argument—that the value-added tax discriminates against firms or industries in which much value-added is created—is fallacious. Ito,[20] for example, mentions as a main disadvantage of the value-added tax that it would discriminate against manufacturing business as compared with sales or brokerage business. While true of a payroll tax, a general value-added tax, like the income tax itself, should not change relative prices,* and should rest on all factors of production in proportion to their incomes.†

An important shortcoming of the value-added tax is that, for administrative reasons, it is not possible to impart to it a progression of the marginal rates. For the time being, let us assume that it is imposed at a flat rate.

From a purely economic and administrative point of view, a proportional income tax has many advantages over a progressive one. Under a proportional income tax the problems of irregular income (including capital gains) and irregular expenditures (including investments) either disappear or lose much of their poignancy, as do the problems of the taxpaying unit and the correct method of taxing corporations. Also, although the economic consequences of even progressive taxes are not necessarily severe, those of proportional taxes are even milder, as should be clear

* That is, in addition to changes in relative prices which are the result of the very decrease in real disposable incomes which is the necessary outcome of the public expenditures.

† Admittedly if the value-added is not accompanied when *first* imposed with a special tax on existing capital goods at the value-added tax rate, there will be a *transition* period in which the value-added tax will discriminate against labor-intensive industries.

from the literature on the effects of taxes on the incentives to effort and risk-taking.* Progression of rates in a general income tax, let us remember, deprives it from some of the merits of generality.

A proportional indirect tax on income—the value-added tax—has most of the advantages of a proportional ordinary income tax, and some more besides. Naturally the concept of income parallel to that of the value-added tax is that of national income (net national product), not that of taxable income which is preferable on grounds of ability to pay. The two categories of income not taxable under a value-added tax are capital gains and transfer payments, including inheritance. Neither should be left untaxed, but, as will be argued shortly, both deserve a "special" tax treatment. The main advantage of the indirect income tax lies in its indirectness which diminishes the psychological costs of taxation. At the same time, it has important advantages over ordinary indirect taxes and even over a truly general sales tax. For one thing, a sales tax is somewhat regressive when compared to incomes, while even a proportional value-added tax is, after all, proportional. The value-added tax is indeed neutral as far as firms are concerned for it changes neither the relative prices of the factors of production nor the relative prices of the products. Not even a general sales tax, not to mention more partial indirect taxes, is neutral in this respect. A general

---

* Special tax abatements offered in the context of incentive taxation also raise less problems when the tax rate is proportional. With a proportional income tax rate, there should certainly be no reason to object to instantaneous depreciation, provided firms pay normal interest on any tax savings as long as they remain extra. Surely the treasury may waive such interest payments and thus increase the profitability of investments in depreciable assets beyond its no-income-tax level. Shoup's consumption type value-added tax, incidentally, implies instantaneous depreciation under the value-added tax.

sales tax as usually conceived is a general consumption tax, and as such it may be superior to an ordinary income tax and to an ordinary value-added tax in its economic effects on households' choice between consumption and savings. But as a general consumption tax, it increases the price of labor more than it does the prices of other factors of production,* and thus becomes distortive at the stage of the use of the primary resources. Also, the political chances of a general sales tax staying general for long seem to be much less than the chances of a value-added tax remaining uniform. Moreover, as a multi-level tax the value-added tax would be superior even to a uniform sales tax on all final expenditures in its economizing effects on production.

Imposing the tax technically on employing the resources should also increase the efficiency in production by eliminating much waste. In this respect the value-added tax has effects directly contrary to those of an income tax. Since expenses are deductible in computing the income tax liability, their real costs to the firms are correspondingly reduced. This does not create distortions when the fruits of the expenditures are taxable, but it does discriminate in favor of such expenditures as luxurious buildings and expensive advertising—both of which generate advantages not purely monetary and thus not fully taxable—and also in favor of expenditures on "fringe benefits" and on "expense accounts" that may decrease more than corresponding payments for wages and salaries. Thus the main disadvantages of "expense accounts" are re-

---

* The consumption tax will raise wage rates either in a Ricardian model, where they are determined by the costs of subsistence, or where wages and salaries are adjusted automatically or in wage negotiations to changes in the costs of living. Since the tax does not apply to capital goods and land, it changes the relative prices of the factors of production.

lated to distorted allocation of resources, not to problems of income distribution.

The value-added tax does not solve all these problems, of course. But unless it is totally shifted to the factors of production, it imposes, for any individual firm, a tax on the employment of any additional unit of any factor, and as such should generate more efficiency at the production level. Instead of taking into account the costs of the wage increases minus the extra saving from income tax, firms should now take the costs of the wage increase plus the extra value-added tax. Thus, imposing the legal act of tax payment on the firms in the economy—which is the essence of a value-added tax—will solve the technical problem of "fringe benefits" and stiffen the resistance of employers to raising wages and salaries. But such problems as "expense accounts" will remain unsolved unless a criterion is found to distinguish between expenses which are part of the compensation of the owners of factors employed by the firms and expenses that are not; but in that case it is an easy problem under ordinary income tax.

From a redistributional point of view, a proportional value-added tax does not compare too badly with the aggregate of total taxes imposed at all levels of government in the United States. Musgrave's computations for 1954 find a rather moderate degree of progression over the lower and middle income ranges and a much steeper progression over the high income brackets range. The estimated effective rates of tax for 1954 start at almost 27 per cent for spending-unit income brackets of $0 to $2,000, move to 28-29 per cent for brackets $2,000 to $5,000 and to 31-33 per cent for brackets $5,000 to $10,000. It is only for income brackets over $10,000 that the effective rate jumps to 40.9 per cent. The general picture,[21] abstracting from the partial progressivity (or regressivity) of the many tax components, is not progressive enough to justify contempt for a proportional tax.* In any case the value-added tax need not and should not be the only tax, so that its "partial progressivity" need not determine the progressivity of the tax system; and, besides, it could be made progressive.

At the cost of some administrative inconvenience, the value-added tax could be made progressive by means of personal and family exemptions. Income-receivers could declare from which source of income they wished their various exemptions to be taken off. And firms would be ready to pay more for the services of, say, an employee, the bigger his family and tax allowances. Thus the exemptions would be readily shifted to the intended beneficiaries and the distributional results achieved. Personal and family exemptions, in spite of the secular decline in their importance, still amounted to 33 per cent of the total adjusted gross income in the U.S.A. in 1955, and have been responsible to a major extent for effective rate progression of the income tax among the great majority of taxpayers. Without personal exemptions, the ratio of income tax to income, in 1953, showed hardly any increase up to $10,000 income.[22]

It is not difficult to incorporate family exemptions for wage and salary earners into a value-added tax. If there is no reliance on the market mechanism of the shifting of the benefits of the exemptions, it is still possible to guarantee, in wage contracts, a family

---

* In his study "How Progressive is the Income Tax?" in *Tax Revision Compendium*, Vol. 3, pp. 2223-33 (Washington, D.C.: Government Printing Office, 1959), Musgrave arrived at the interesting conclusion that if income splitting were abolished, realized capital gains and unrealized gains at time of death fully taxable, tax exempt interest and percentage depletion eliminated, wage supplements included in taxable income, and deductions disallowed, actual tax at incomes exceeding one million dollars would be only 24 per cent, which is also their level on adjusted gross incomes of $25,000 to $50,000.

wage increase which will be equal, per dependent, to the value for the employer of the additional exemption he is allowed from the value-added tax. Similar mechanisms may work with sources of incomes other than wages and salaries. Yet the most sensible—and most progressive—method of solving this problem is by means of family grants paid by the treasury to taxpayers and non-taxpayers alike. Such grants, like tax exemptions themselves, may also serve demographic or other social goals. Indeed, this arrangement has important advantages over ordinary tax exemptions in that they are given also to those too poor to benefit from tax exemptions; and, since their benefits are quite obvious, they should also improve the public-relations standing of the government.

Still, exemptions need not be considered the only source of progressivity. The value-added tax should not obtain fiscal monopoly. For one thing, as a tax on income from selling economic services it obviously does not fall on capital gains and transfer receipts; but clearly there is no reason to leave such income untaxed. From a purely economic standpoint, transfer receipts are ideal subjects for taxation as no substitution effects whatsoever need be dreaded. Nor should serious problems of tax effects on incentives arise in the case of bona fide capital gains. Although tax exempt in many countries, incomes from lotteries, for example, could be taxed heavily without any ill-effects to the economy, and indeed it would be logical to do so before resorting to more harmful ways of taxation. Indeed it is suggested here that both capital and "windfall" gains and transfer receipts—including inheritances and gifts—should be taxed at a rate higher than that of the value-added tax, 30 to 35 per cent making good sense to me.* The "punitive" rate on such

---

* Exemptions should be given to persons for whom such incomes are the only source of income and who thus do not benefit from exemptions under the value-added tax.

incomes would eliminate many forms of capital gains
which are but legal forms of ordinary incomes resulting from the current lenient tax treatment of capital
gains. Such incomes—often plain interest and profits
—should not and will not bear any extra tax. The tax
on capital gains should apply to all forms of realized
gains, considering unrealized gains at time of death
as realized. The only valid argument against ordinary
taxation of such incomes—their irregularity—loses its
punch when the tax is imposed at a single rate. If the
tax system includes a property tax of the net-worth
type, as it should, tax revenues of this particular tax
will rise when unrealized capital gains occur.

With a net-worth tax, capital gains (and losses)
should be reported annually. Thus from an administrative point of view a net-worth tax facilitates adminis-
tering the special capital-gains tax, and also a transfer-
receipts tax.

In the field of ordinary outlay taxes, there is room
for tariffs at a rate not below that of the value-added
tax. Actually, customs-free trade will involve at a
given exchange rate a clear misallocation of resources
from a national point of view when all internal transactions are subject to a value-added tax. Other specific functions of outlay taxes, like taxing dissavings,
will be fulfilled by the tax on value-added itself.

There is no reason why an ordinary income tax, a
kind of a sur-tax, should not be also imposed on top
of the value-added tax and the special tax on capital
gains and transfer receipts.* The sur-tax should be
definitely progressive, but though its progression may
be quite steep, its absolute rate will be much lower
than the current income tax rates. This sur-tax—with

---

* Admittedly, wherever the value-added tax consists mainly
of rewards for entrepreneurship or professional knowledge, the
difference between an ordinary income tax and the value-added
tax would be slight to begin with.

no loopholes—will probably play only a limited fiscal role; but, on the other hand, with pre-World War II rate schedules, it should have very limited economic costs.

Such a tax system, we believe, might substantially reduce the psychological costs of taxation without reducing its effective progressivity. To be sure, whether this belief is justified or not does not lie within the sphere of economics proper, and this may rightly reduce its interest for economists. Let us explain, therefore, that although our discussion has been in terms of the U.S. tax system, our tax plan is suggested mainly for countries with systems which are less developed, less progressive, and more distortive, and with fiscal needs more urgent, and where taxpayers' objections to increased taxation jeopardizes the very process of development.

NOTES

1. See Ursala H. Hicks, "The Terminology of Tax Analysis," *The Economic Journal*, Vol. LVI, No. 221 (March 1946), reprinted in *Readings in the Economics of Taxation*, selected by Richard A. Musgrave and Carl S. Shoup (Homewood, Illinois: Irwin), pp. 214-26.

2. Carl S. Shoup, "Some Problems in the Incidence of the Corporation Income Tax," *American Economic Review, Papers and Proceedings*, Vol. L, No. 2 (May 1960), pp. 458-60.

3. Cf. Robert Ferber, "How Aware Are Consumers of Excise Tax Changes?" *National Tax Journal*, Vol. VII (December 1954), pp. 355-58.

4. Cf. C. E. Axelson, *The History of Taxation in Natal*,

Prior to Union (unpublished thesis, Natal University College, Durban, 1936), pp. 88-90.

5. For a good exposition and rationalization, see James Tobin, "Money Wage Rates and Employment," *The New Economics,* ed. by Seymour E. Harris, (New York: Knopf, 1948), pp. 579-81.

6. Cf. A. J. Brown, *The Great Inflation 1939-1951* (New York: Oxford University Press, 1955), pp. 200-25.

7. George Katona, *Psychological Analysis of Economic Behavior* (New York: McGraw-Hill, 1951), pp. 88-90.

8. See Anthony Downs, *An Economic Theory of Democracy* (New York: Harper, 1957).

9. *Ibid.,* p. 255.

10. Cf. Talcott Parsons, Edward A. Shils, and James Olds, "Values, Motives and Systems of Action," in *Toward a General Theory of Action* (Cambridge, Massachusetts: Harvard University Press, 1952), pp. 53-109, esp. pp. 80-88.

11. Katona, *op. cit.,* pp. 36-40.

12. *Ibid.,* p. 38.

13. Cf. M. Bronfenbrenner, "Some Neglected Implications of Secular Inflation," *Post Keynesian Economics,* ed. by Kenneth K. Kurihara (New Brunswick, N.J.: Rutgers University Press, 1959), pp. 31-58.

14. See G. Schmölders, "Fiscal Psychology: A New Branch of Public Finance," *National Tax Journal,* Vol. XII (December 1959), pp. 340-45.

15. The importance of psychological factors, and of the Italian contribution to research in this field, is stressed by James N. Buchanan, *Fiscal Theory and Political Economy* (Chapel Hill, North Carolina: University of North Carolina Press, 1960).

16. Cf. John Kenneth Galbraith, *The Affluent Society* (London: Hamish Hamilton, 1958), pp. 245-50.

17. Cf. Richard A. Musgrave, *The Theory of Public Finance* (New York: McGraw-Hill, 1959), pp. 350-53.

18. *Ibid.,* p. 378.

The equivalence of the two taxes is pointed out by Carl Shoup, "Theory and Background of the Value-Added Tax," in *Proceedings of the 48th Conference of the National Tax Association* (Sacramento, California, 1956), pp. 6-19. Other references are mentioned in the bibliographical note to this article, pp. 18-19.

19. *Ibid.*, p. 13.

20. Cf. Hanya Ito, "The Value-Added Tax in Japan," in his *Essays in Public Finance* (Tokyo, Japan: The Science Council of Japan, 1954) pp. 32-33.

21. See Richard A. Musgrave, "The Incidence of the Tax Structure and Its Effects on Consumption," in *Federal Tax Policy for Economic Growth and Stability* (Washington, D.C.: Government Printing Office, 1956), pp. 96-113, and the summary Table 2, p. 98.

22. See C. Harry Kahn, *Personal Deductions in the Federal Income Tax* (Princeton, N.J.: Princeton University Press, 1960), pp. 25-28.

CHAPTER SEVEN

INFLATION
AS A TAX

An indirect income tax has all the advantages of indirectness but all its disadvantages as well, mainly its price-raising character which is rightly resented as inflationary.

Inflation itself has many definitions, some in terms of causes, others in terms of symptoms. Indeed, not only are there numerous definitions but numerous inflations as well, some pulled by demand, some pushed by costs, some associated with an unduly large increase in money supply, some with a decline in the physical volume of transactions, some open, some galloping, some repressed fully or partly, some designed, some accidental, some originated in the financial sector, some upheld by the financial sector in spite of its resentment, some resulting from deficit financing of some government expenditures, and some more privately created.

It is customary to view inflations as bad, and usually they are. But since there are many kinds, it is not easy to generalize. It is clear, however, that inflations do change an agreed-upon distribution of income, mainly at the expense of people whose incomes are either absolutely or relatively fixed in money terms, and impose an excise on the holding of money balances and other assets with rather rigid "prices." Inflation may also seriously dampen the incentives to work, save, and invest; distort the composition of investments, encouraging as it does speculative investments which are not socially productive; encourage flight of capital to foreign countries as a hedge against itself; and have other serious consequences which the literature on the subject describes more than adequately.

Inflation is clearly a very indirect tax and as such has all the psychological advantage of indirectness, and deficit financing may, at the margin, be a justifiable means of finance even in prosperous economies. As argued in Chapter 1, the comparison between the various taxes should always be made at the margin, and it is not self-evident that the marginal social costs of inflation would always exceed those of alternative methods of finance either from a distribution-of-income point of view or in its distortive effects on the allocation of resources. Recent studies of the mild inflation that took place in the United States between 1939 and 1952 indicate that there is little evidence that it reduced the real output of society, or significantly changed the size distribution of incomes between rich and poor or between Labor and Capital.[1] While not necessarily true of other inflations, these results indicate that indeed, as a tax, inflation need not always be inferior at the margin to other methods of finance.

The two special characteristics of inflation which distinguish it from ordinary taxes are not its evil results but, first, that it is not imposed by the legislative body; and secondly, that its revenues do not go exclusively to the government but are partly dissipated almost blindly to the benefiting private groups.[2]

It is an historical fact that, while the legislative body has been stubborn in refusing to delegate much power to the fiscal authorities so that legislative approval is needed even for minor changes in tax laws and rates, extensive delegation of power to the central bank has been orthodox. Indeed, one of the advantages often ascribed to monetary policy, in contradiction to fiscal policy, is that monetary authorities are relatively free from legislative intervention and thus are more flexible. This is not to say that monetary measures do not inflict capital gains and losses. They do. In addition, they may affect—via changes in money supply—both the size of national income and its distribution. But nonetheless it has been found essential to exclude them from direct legislative supervision. Indeed, in many countries the central bank has acquired a special status which in some ways resembles that of the judiciary. In its common stand against inflation, the monetary authorities "have become the protectors of a particular social group—the unorganized fixed income receivers."[3] But while this may sound justified, it is not at all clear why society should waive its control over monetary policy.*

---

* It is often argued that monetary policy may be left relatively uncontrolled, for, unlike fiscal policy, monetary control is impersonal and nondiscriminatory. But even general, not to mention selective, credit control is administered through the personal decisions of bankers on personal requests for credit.

Monetary policy and fiscal policy are clearly two instruments by which the government can achieve its financial goals, and as two branches they may both complement or substitute each other.* Controlling the one without the other necessarily involves giving up much of the government's power to control. The major disadvantage of the freedom of the monetary sector, however, is not that it prevents the imposition of some taxes possibly against the opinion of the majority, but that it is free to impose major taxes against the wish of society which may be quite ignorant of their imposition.

Inflation is a tax which could not exist in a barter economy, and as such it is ultimately imposed by the monetary authorities without conscious legislative approval. This, I believe, is the major shortcoming of inflation as a tax. Substitute for inflation a recurrent tax on money and bond holdings and on fixed incomes, and you will get most of the effects of inflation. Legislative approval will not turn this tax into a good one, but it will turn it into just one of the many inequitable and distortive taxes.

The second distinctive characteristic of inflation as a tax is that its revenues do not go exclusively to the government. As a monetary phenomenon, inflation could not occur in a barter economy, but it easily could happen in an economy with no government. In a governed economy, inflation may be generated either by the private or by the public sector or by both, and its benefits may be shared by the government and by a part of the private sector. Since inflation redistributes incomes and wealth from those whose incomes and net worths rise *less* than the price level to those whose

---

* In many cases, tax devices are intended to affect the rate of interest which applies to business decisions. See Richard Goode, "Accelerated Depreciation Allowances as a Stimulus to Investments," *Quarterly Journal of Economics,* Vol. LXIX (May 1955), pp. 191-211.

incomes and net worths rise *more*, it is obvious that inflation will have supporters in the private sector who benefit from it either directly or because it reduces their tax burden. Colin Clark's thesis on the limits of taxation is indeed based on the relative strength of inflationary pressure groups in all economies.

In short, we believe that these two special characteristics of inflation are its major disadvantages, and are sufficient to justify its rejection even when mild or creeping.

In a conference held by the International Economic Association,[4] several participants objected to inflation not because of its effects on the growth of national income, or its distribution among factor shares or income groups, or on the balance of payments, but because it damages money as a unit of value. Indeed, several distinguished economists expressed their opinion at the conference that keeping the purchasing-power of a unit of money constant, or even increasing it with increases in productivity, should be an established overriding norm for financial policy, fixed perhaps even by law. I have little sympathy with this viewpoint. For me, inflation is evil only because it imposes an arbitrary tax and imparts arbitrary subsidies, because it may have distortive effects on the allocation of resources, because it will create—at fixed exchange rates—balance-of-payments problems, because it may affect the propensity to save, and so forth. In short, to me, the costs of inflation consist mainly of effects on the size of the real product, its growth, and its distribution. A rising price level as such—were its only effect to reduce the purchasing-power of the unit of money (and if this had no other consequences) —might be quite satisfying to those suffering from money illusion, including perhaps many labor union leaders, but for many others, including myself, it would be a nuisance. Yet surely this should be one of the least important worries of a government attempting to protect the true interests of the economy. In a closed economy, a decreasing price level (with no unemployment or any other consequences) does not seem to be superior to a rising one; it is the permanent change which is annoying. In an open economy, a different rate of change in the price level in the various countries taking part in international trade would necessitate changes in the rates of exchange. But such results—which I do not consider terribly serious—are, as a matter of fact, caused by the effects of inflation on the balance of payments.

The base of the inflation tax consists of the value of all financial assets with a constant nominal redemption value (mainly money and bonds) and all nominally constant money incomes, like—and this differs from one economy to another—wages and salaries, interest payments, rents, pensions, and social security receipts. Thus, in a modern economy, the tax imposed by inflation on the government's own employees and beneficiaries may be quite sizable. Indeed, if the tax system has built-in flexibility, so that the money revenues of taxation rise more than proportionately to the rise in money incomes, inflation again increases, although indirectly, the resources available for government use.[5] Even the intraprivate sector transfers of incomes and wealth brought about by inflation may be resource-releasing if the marginal propensity to spend of those who gain by inflation is smaller than that of those who lose by it. Inflation "works" by reducing the purchasing-power of constant money incomes—to the extent that they remain constant—and may be specially "efficient" if those incomes are derived from government expenditures.

Of special importance, and a source of misunderstanding, is the effect of inflation on real money balances. In his "Discussion of the Inflationary Gap,"[6] Milton Friedman analyzed the means by which this gap may be closed in an open inflation. He mentioned the roles of frictions and lags in bringing about changes in relative prices and incomes which, depending on the spending-saving relationships in the various sectors of the economy, may reduce total demand for resources; but special attention was paid to another deflationary factor—the very rise in the price level itself. Friedman recognizes explicitly that the rise in prices is also a rise in incomes, so that, in the absence of special assumptions, a rise in prices cannot reduce aggregate demand through its effect on real incomes. But, he points out, the rise in the price level also reduces the real value of the initial stock of money, and therefore if people wish to replenish their real balances either partly or fully, they must reduce their demand for goods and services and thus somewhat reduce the inflationary gap.

Consequently, when there is no further expansion in money supply, the inflationary increase in the price level is deflationary. The bigger the reduction in real balances, the greater the burden of inflation as a tax. But paradoxically, reductions in real balances also represent increases in the demands for goods and services on the part of the public. The less the decrease in real balances for a given amount of deficit financing, the more resources the government receives for it. Nonetheless, reductions in real balances do play an important role in closing inflationary gaps.

It has recently been suggested that the inflation tax could be measured by the inflation-induced cut in real balances. But by doing so, one would have abstracted from the other effects just mentioned, and also created the mistaken impression that the higher the increase in the price level, the more efficient is inflation as a tax, whereas, as a matter of fact, a galloping inflation may, from the government's point of view, be quite functionless. In any case, it should be stressed that the part of the inflation tax represented by the reduction in the real value of money balances (less bank loans) and government bonds should be measured by changes in the real value of the amounts outstanding at the *beginning* of the period,[7] or, rather, with a period of a finite length, the comparison should be made between the correctly averaged balances for the period under consideration and the correctly weighted average rise in the price level. In any event, it makes no sense to multiply the amount outstanding at the end of the period, which includes the additions to money and government debt that brought about the inflation, by the rate of price increase that took place.*

DEFICIT FINANCING

Before going further, it might help to clarify matters to distinguish between deficit financing and inflation. The amount of resources that the government gets by deficit finance naturally depends on the price level within the period; the higher the rise in prices, the smaller the resources received by the government by a given amount of deficit finance. If private groups can also increase the money supply by borrowing from financial institutions (under a permissive monetary policy), it is not even necessary that inflation will be functional at all from the point of view of the government. That is, it is not at all certain that the

---

* It would be possible, and I would like to see it realized, to devise an inflation-proof economy by escalating everything, including all or any assets and liabilities, to a price index chosen for this purpose. Such a plan—to be discussed very soon in some detail—would protect everyone from the *effects* of rising prices; but, naturally, prices might continue to rise, and their rise might even be accelerated. Although nobody pays a tax, and although real balances are not depleted—for the holders of cash balances are fully compensated for any price increase— inflation as a tax measured by the rate of price increase times money balances and government debt at the end of the period may reach very high, but completely misleading, heights.

government will get any additional resources by means of "printing money." Indeed, it is conceivable that the marginal real value for the government of the "new" money issued in some period of time will be zero or negative.[8] With a fractional reserve banking system it cannot be taken for granted that the government will necessarily always be ahead of the race. Not only will private borrowers not always lag after the government, but with expectations of the next government move, they may very well anticipate it.* If, as is currently believed in some quarters, monetary policy is not as potent as is claimed by some economists— because of the existence of substitute means of payments which cannot be controlled by the ordinary monetary instruments—then the "inflation game" may be lost by the government even when it does its best to win it.

A functionless inflation, from the government's standpoint, does not imply a burdenless inflation; it implies only that money gains of one part of the private sector are exactly equal to the money losses of its other part—an equality which, needless to say, does not mean equality in utility terms.

If an attempt is made to measure the incidence of inflation as a tax, the best approach would probably be to compare what happens between the beginning of the period and its end to the size and distribution of real disposable incomes, real private consumption, and real—that is, adjusted for changes in the price

---

* The possibility of being functionless is not limited to inflation; it is also true of taxes. The very existence of taxes is not in itself proof that somebody actually suffers from them. Taxes may be functionless even when they are not meant to be, as are, for example, taxes that are fully compensated for in adjustments in incomes and net assets. In economies where wages are escalated to cost-of-living indices, and where constant-purchasing-power bonds are gaining in popularity, the relative or absolute sterility of some taxes as resource-releasers may be taken for granted.

level—net worths of individuals. Limitations of a detailed study of the incidence of inflation as a tax among income brackets or income sources depend only on the limitations of the existing statistical data. Any group with reduced real expenditures on consumption or on additions to physical assets gives up resources, either voluntarily or compulsorly, while the contrary is true of any group with increased real expenditures on consumption and additions to physical assets. Voluntary increases in financial assets (again, correctly deflated) should be offset against cuts in private consumption and investment, as a matter of course. They may release resources for public use as much as involuntary increases, but they should not affect the welfare of those who bought them.

In more detail, if a constant (and equal) marginal propensity to spend is assumed, and if the government gains are abstracted from reduced real payments and if the measured inflation tax is to include the inflation-induced gains of private net borrowers, firms, or households as if they were designed public transfers to those parties—and it is important to make these reservations—then the total inflation tax should be measured by the increase in money supply deflated by the increase in the price level minus increases (or plus decreases) in the value of the real money balances and government bonds held by the public. This may be clearer if viewed not as the gain of the government—for it is not self-evident why a decrease in real cash balances should make the government more comfortable*—but as the losses of the private sector.

---

* Is it not the lack of symmetry between the economic effect of an increase in the price level on the money-issuing authorities on one hand, and on money-holders on the other, that is the very source of the phenomenon called real balance effects? That a decrease in the real value of government bonds held by the public benefits the government is clear enough.

Suppose the increase in money supply generates no rise in the price level; in this case an increase will obtain in the amount of real balances voluntarily held.* Such a rise in real balances or in the real value of government bonds will impose no burden on its holders who chose to direct a part of their savings to this purpose. On the other hand, if a decrease obtains in the real value of government bonds and money balances held by the public, without an offsetting increase in its other assets, its net worth will be reduced, and this clearly will constitute a burden. Only if there is no change in the sum of real balances and government bonds—that is, only if the price level rises proportionately to the increase in government debt and money supply—will the total gross inflation burden on the private sector be equal, under the assumptions mentioned above, to the amount of resources released by it to the government.†

If, on the other hand, the tax imposed by inflation for the government's own use is to be distinguished from the inflation tax imposed by private expansion in money supply, one should compute the inflation

---

* If the increase in real balances is not voluntary, as in a truly repressed inflation, it may be legitimately argued that the price-level index is understated in not reflecting the infinite prices of unavailable goods.

† Cagan defines the revenues of inflation in real terms per period of time as the sum of two parts; first, the real value of new money issued per period of time, $\dfrac{-dM}{dt}\,\dfrac{1}{P}$, plus the decrease (or minus the increase) per period of time in the real value of cash balances, $\dfrac{d\left(\dfrac{M}{P}\right)}{dt}$. See Philip Cagan, "The Monetary Dynamics of Hyperinflation," *Studies in the Quantity Theory of Money* (edited by Milton Friedman), (Chicago: The University of Chicago Press, 1956), pp. 25-117 and esp. p. 78.

tax, under the assumptions, by measuring the amount of resources obtained by deficit financing plus the decrease (minus the increase) in the sum of the real value of government bonds plus money supply *minus* bank loans to the public, the latter constituting the privately generated increase in money supply.

Let us stress that although inflation imposes, by definition, a tax on holding a unit of money and bonds, it does not necessarily reduce the demand for real balances held. Clearly, by increasing their price, inflation does reduce the demand for real balances. Yet the very process of inflation itself depends on an increase in the supply of money balances.*

To be sure, since continuing increases in the price level will sooner or later be part of general expectations, the transactions velocity of money will rise, so that the price level will ultimately rise more than proportionately to the increase in money supply, and real money balances will be reduced. But this may very

---

* That real balances may increase during inflation is very well known. Indeed, such an increase is probably the most conspicuous feature of a successfully repressed inflation. John J. Klein's "German Money and Prices, 1932-44," in *Studies in the Quantity Theory of Money*, pp. 119-59, compares, in effect, the relative *increases* in real balances that took place in Germany, Italy, the United Kingdom, and the United States during World War II and some years before the war and after it. The index of real cash balances in Germany in 1944 was 440.2 (1932 = 100). The height of the German increase in real balances may be puzzling, but the very increase itself is almost the natural result of repressing an inflation. Indeed, the essence of completely repressed inflations is that the inflationary savings take the form of additions to private net worths, and this situation holds as long as price remains repressed. Repressed inflations are, obviously, nonequilibrium conditions, and prices will ultimately rise. This rise of prices will indeed reduce real balances, and, indirectly, reduce the demand for resources in the period during which it occurs. A sometimes drastic cut in real balance is, on the other hand, typical of all hyper-inflation, as the studies of such inflations clearly indicate.

well happen long after the period when the inflation-released resources have been used by the government.

TOWARD AN INFLATION-PROOF ECONOMY

Inflation inflicts important social losses even when it does not exist. Indeed the very fear of inflation may itself be extremely costly. As T. V. Houser noted in 1958: "Inflation's evil can even be found in the current recession. Action to fight the decline was inhibited by fear of contributing to inflation in the future. So once again, it is revealed as the enemy of stable growth."[9] This quotation is not unique. Indeed, the literature on fiscal policy often stresses the difficulties of correct timing, and the dangers of promoting one evil while fighting its opposite. It follows that the costs of inflation are not operative exclusively in terms of undesirable changes in income distribution and in the allocation of resources, but, indirectly, by means of the very fear of inflation, also in terms of the level of production itself. In this regard, Samuelson and Solow estimate that, in the United States, price stability would involve 7 or 8 per cent unemployment, instead of the 2 or 3 per cent that are necessary because of unavoidable frictions.[10] A. P. Lerner concludes that because of much part-time work and job protection, the reduction of output would be of the order of magnitude of 30 to 50 billion dollars, at the G.N.P. 1960 level.[11] This compares with 35.6 billion dollars, the individual income tax yield in 1958, and with 26 billion dollars, the budget expenditures in 1957 of the Federal Government on international affairs and finance, veterans' services and benefits, labor and welfare, agriculture and agricultural resources, national resources, commerce and housing, and interest and general government—that is, all budget expenditures of the Federal Government with the exception of

expenditures on national security. This cost may far
exceed the costs of the inflation that might have taken
place had there been less fear of it. Quite obviously,
it is very important to find a way to get rid of inflation, and in this section I shall discuss a proposal
that may indeed deprive inflation of most of its evils.

But before going into it, I should first explain why,
having stressed the importance of fiscal psychology,
I do not give sufficient credit to the psychological
advantages of inflation as a tax. For, after all, as a tax
that is never openly imposed, it does have important
psychological advantages even when compared to indirect taxes. Yet, as I have mentioned, the psychological advantages of any tax should never be the
determining factor in its choice as a means of finance;
thus, for example, even though excises are probably
less "noticeable" than the value-added tax suggested
in Chapter 5, they still have important economic
shortcomings.[12] Secondly, I have not meant to suggest
that the legislative body itself should not be conscious
of the imposition of taxes, as indeed it is not in the case
of inflation where it is not even formally consulted.
Thirdly, the intraprivate sector transfers brought
about by inflation must be considered as one of its
major disadvantages; since, being arbitrary, they cannot be equitable. In a specious contradiction to the
attitude expressed in Chapter 5, it is suggested here
that if the taxes administered by inflation are considered to be at the margin of lower social costs than
their alternatives, they should be imposed openly.

Without surveying the costs of inflation, it may be
stated generally that it is the change in relative
prices, if such a change takes place, not that in
absolute prices, which is the source of both the evils
of inflation to those who suffer from it and its blessings
to those that gain by it. Neither consequence would
occur, however, if *all* prices rose to the same extent.

That is, if prices of skilled and unskilled labor rose at the same rate as do prices paid for supply of capital, both risky and relatively safe, then nothing at all would happen to the distribution of incomes. Something does happen, of course, to the value of a unit of money,[13] but for the moment let us disregard that. In practice, however, some prices are contractually fixed, or at least somewhat rigid, so that relative prices do change when inflation occurs. And, it is the change in *relative* prices that impoverishes workers, or rentiers, or holders of cash and bank deposits, or pensioners, or whoever gets a contractual or semi-contractual payment. Needless to say, this very impoverishment must benefit somebody else, either in governmental or in other sectors. The allocational effects of inflation, good and/or bad, also depend on changes in relative rather than in absolute prices. Inflation may certainly cut savings or investments, it may certainly change the occupational distribution, and it may certainly direct energies in search of hedges, including capital flights abroad, against inflation.

Since inflation does keep rearing its ugly head, it is only natural for its victims to look for protective methods, among which are escalating wages and salaries to a price index agreed upon in employment contracts;[14] and, for the benefit of unearned incomes, issues of constant-purchasing-power bonds.[15] Arrangements like these have become more and more common; wages have been at least partly automatically escalated to cost-of-living or similar indices in Chile, Denmark, Finland, France, Israel, Italy, Norway, and in some branches of industry in England, while in the U.S.A., the use of sliding-scale agreements has been limited to a proportionately small fraction of the working class.[16] The use of constant-purchasing-power bonds is still rather circumscribed, despite the declared support of W. Stanley Jevons, Alfred Marshall, Irving Fisher, Milton Friedman, Fritz Machlup, Sumner Slichter, and many other economists in other countries.[17] In his survey on this subject, Finch mentions opposition to the idea not only by financial experts, like Sir Otto Niemeyer of the Bank of England, and by business economists, but also by Walter Bagehot in 1875, and by the Treasury and the Council of Economic Advisors in 1952. Nor has this opposition subsided.[18]

Indeed, although changes in cost-of-living indices are naturally an important factor in wage negotiations wherever they take place, even wage escalations have come under the attack not only by inflation-oriented pressure groups, but by economists who tend to object to such devices on the grounds that they start or accelerate a wage-price spiral and thus hurt the defenseless sectors. Naturally the more galloping the inflation, the closer the unprotected sectors approach destruction. It is certainly a legitimate criticism of plans to protect specific sectors or groups from inflation that the costs involved might be paid by other inflation victims rather than by the beneficiaries. But, actually, the prospects for an acceleration of inflation decrease when protection becomes *general*, for there is less *motivation* to inflate. In any case, a quicker inflation, *mutatis mutandis*, does not necessarily imply a worse one. Moreover, while interpersonal utility comparisons must be made before partial protection plans can legitimately be either condemned or recommended, no such comparisons would be needed for a wholehearted endorsement of schemes for a general protection against inflation. Indeed, what is suggested here is that, unless explicitly denied in contracts, all contractual payments be escalated to a price index agreed upon for the purpose.

If this were done, all receivers of wages, salaries,

rents, interest, pensions, and other transfer payments —all income payments that were agreed upon in exact and definite money units—would be protected against inflation. All that is required would be a contract clause stating that all money payments explicitly stated be related to a given date, and be adjusted according to a conversion factor derived from a price index agreed upon for this purpose. Indeed, the experience of many countries indicate that wages, salaries, and pensions could be protected from inflation with comparative ease. But it would not be sufficient to protect income payments only; all payments, including capital payments, would need to be submitted to the same kind of escalation. In spite of much critical talk—based mainly on some particularly unfortunate forms of escalation or on attempts of some governments to rig the price index or to evade in other ways their obligations—the experience of other countries indicates that constant-purchasing-power bonds are not impractical. Indeed, under a system where automatic protection from inflation is offered to everyone who wishes it, they lose most of their disadvantages. Both interest and principal values should be escalated, with the market price at any particular moment determined by the market, which will continue to regulate the price of equities and nonescalated bonds. The same arrangement should cover bank loans and deposits, and, it is suggested here, also money notes. For if money balances are not protected from inflation, there will still be an excise imposed on them.

No technical difficulty need arise in protecting bank deposits not in excess of bank loans. Since bank loans will also be escalated—unless banks choose, at their own risk, not to use the escalation clause—it will be simple to compensate those who lend to the banks. This will be achieved by transfer payments, managed by the banks, from those who need bank loans to those who ultimately provide them with the flow of funds. The escalation of bank deposits created by bank loans will not increase money supply, since the loans will be escalated as well, and when they are repaid there will be a decrease either in bank deposits or in the money notes in circulation.

It would be unfair to demand that the government compensate holders of money which it has not created. The protection of money notes plus the excess of bank deposits over bank loans raises important difficulties. As Friedman has made clear, it is the decline in the value of real balances that ultimately closes the inflationary gap, so that increasing money balances whenever the price level rises will deprive the system of its equilibrating factor. True, under the circumstances, inflation will be harmless; but if any fall in the value of a unit of money will be made out by an increase in its nominal value, the increase in the price level will be infinite. Money will turn into an abstract accounting unit, and the economy will return to the barter stage. A completely escalated system, as described, would give a death blow to inflation, but, alas, it would also destroy the monetary system.

The results will be quite different, however, if the compensation for the debtors of the public sector is not made by money creation. Just as private borrowers cannot be assured of meeting their increased nominal liabilities by getting increased loans from the banking system, the public sector itself should do its best to meet the increased nominal liabilities out of budget revenues excluding the inflation tax. Since, under the circumstances, the government is the only beneficiary of inflation even when it is not its generator, it should repay the unintended inflation tax. The revenues for this purpose may come out of increased tax revenues which will occur either due to built-in flexibility of the tax system, or out of increased taxes which may include, if it is so decided, designed taxes on those whom the scheme attempts to protect.

Technically, the escalation of money notes should be made much easier through the banking system,* so that the more developed the banking system the easier it will be to implement the plan. It is sensible to expect, however, that if the increase in the price level does become considerable, people will protect their money balances by depositing them, even for very short periods, in banks in anticipation of the escalation.

The plan as presented here is a maximum plan. For the sake of administrative feasibility, it would be possible to modify it slightly without killing its essence. For example, the adjustments in bank deposits could be made only once a year, adding up, monthly, the losses of depositors according to their average balances in that month and the rate of price increase that occurred then, thus avoiding the effects on expectations of haphazard compensations for inflationary losses of holders of bank deposits. If there is a net-worth tax, compensation should be given for the rate of price increase minus the rate of that tax, or minus a rate of price increase determined by the legislative body as an intended tax on money balances.

All this may seem like a nuisance, and indeed would be—especially in relation to currency notes. But it might prove to be much less of a nuisance than it seems. Unless the inflation is galloping, changes in the inflation-measuring price index may have to be computed only several times a year or even less, as mentioned above. The plan certainly strengthens the cost-push elements of inflation, but as we have noted, there are factors working in the other direction, such

---

* Alternatively, and much more clumsily, money notes will need a special treatment invoking the use of a special "date" when they are imprinted.

as the lack of motivation to inflate if it is realized that nobody is going to win (or lose) by it, or the lack of inflation-induced and inflation-creating increases in the velocity of circulation. But even considerable nuisance should be compared with the benefits involved, which, tautologically, should equal the net costs of inflation. How many billions of dollars worth of benefits are sufficient to justify the costs?

Admittedly, the rise of prices in an inflation-proof economy may (though does not have to) be very high. This price rise, however, would be devoid of distributional and allocational effects. Most importantly, recessions in this economy would probably be much briefer and milder, for here no fiscal or monetary measure against recession (which may take only the form of a decline in the rate of growth of product) would have to be used hesitatingly because of worries lest it overshoot the mark and generate the other evil, inflation. Inflation, in short, would have lost its terror.

Is anything wrong with this scheme of sterile or functionless inflation? Opposition to it might be based on conservatism (in the sense of objection to changes), misunderstandings, sheer partisanship, or on intrinsic weaknesses of the scheme. Strongest resistance might come from those who condemn inflation but who would hate to see it go. That there are sectors in the economy that do benefit from inflation is only the mirror image of the distributional effects of inflation, whatever they may be. The beneficiaries usually consist of profit-receivers and net debtors, and may very well include the government, including the legislative bodies. As is well known, inflation is a convenient tool to lighten the burden of all domestic obligations that are stated in money terms, like interest payments and redemption of national debt, social security and pension payments, and civil service salaries.[19] Moreover, as a financing device, inflation has—at least when mild—some obvious psychological comparative advantages, so that the temptation to use it might, on occasion, be almost irresistible. Yet it is hard to think of an effect of inflation that could not be elicited by other premeditated policies. I do not think that inflation has no alternatives whatsoever. Indeed, if economies cannot win wars or develop without inflation, why all the talk of the evils of something society cannot do without.

Some objections to the scheme might be based on preference for inflationless rather than inflation-proof economies. But nothing in the scheme prevents strict anti-inflationary policies; it only makes the consequences of a failure of such policies much less important socially.

Resistance might also gather around the inadequacy of any price index for the purpose of general protection against inflation. Ideally, to be sure, one would have to construct a special index for almost every individual, but that is obviously impossible. The index used should be a general index of prices, like the cost-of-living index, measuring in some sense changes in the value of money. It should definitely *not* be the index of the prices of some specific commodities, including gold or foreign exchange. Some supposedly constant-purchasing-power bonds are escalated to the value of gold or to the exchange rate of some foreign currencies. This seems to me to be disadvantageous from many points of view.

First, in this case there is indeed some form of "abdication of the local currency," which may be demoralizing. Secondly, escalation to such an index does not at all achieve what is supposedly needed; the moral case for adjusting payments because of devaluations (or appreciations) of the external value of a currency seems doubtful unless there are changes in the internal value as well. Thirdly, since it is unlikely that escalation will depend on exchange rates in some nonofficial markets, and since official exchange rates do not change very often, many problems are created by the greater role played here by the time element. Many inequities may be completed between devaluations; there would be quite a burden on, say, anyone who borrowed shortly before a devaluation took place, and no help at all for debtors who happened to lend just after a devaluation took place and got paid back just before one. Fear of such cases might create some nerve-racking speculations and thus make agreements much more difficult to achieve. Moreover, the whole system might be short-lived because, due to misunderstandings, the public may lose its confidence in it. Owners of long-term bonds might find out, disappointingly, that the market value of their bonds does not necessarily rise in proportion to the rate of devaluation. Even if redemption did ultimately take place at a price that would fully compensate for devaluation, the market price just after a devaluation would be determined by discounting the redemption price according to the length of time still to be waited, and according to the excess of interest paid on non-linked bonds over that paid on the linked ones. Such discount might be high indeed; if five more years have to pass after devaluation before redemption can occur, and if the excess of interest paid on ordinary bonds over that paid on gold (or foreign exchange) bonds is, say, 8 per cent, the market value of the bonds just after devaluation will be only 68 per cent of redemption value. This is certainly not cheating, but a layman might very well view it as such.

Another, and important, reason against the choice of such methods of escalation is that economic conditions might require changing the rate of exchange. It seems silly to try to prevent changes that have to take place in relative prices, yet no devaluation could be

effective in a foreign exchange escalated system.*
Similar objections might be raised against the use of
a wage index, suggested by Professor Pedersen of
Denmark, for constant-purchasing-power bonds. Pedersen's idea was to assure savers of the constancy

* The Israeli experience is illuminating in this respect. Linkage of loans either to the cost-of-living index or to the foreign
exchange rate have been common, and have been growing in
importance, in Israel since 1955. In 1961 bonds linked to the
dollar constituted 44.3 per cent of the par-value of all Israeli
securities registered in the stock exchange, while bonds linked
to the cost-of-living index amounted to 10.6 per cent; 11.4 per
cent were linked, with equal weights, to the cost-of-living index
and to the exchange rate of the dollar. Thus 66.3 per cent of
all Israeli securities were at the time linked to either or both
bases. On the other hand, the development budget loans
granted by the government to various private sectors were, on
the eve of the devaluation of the currency on February 9, 1962,
mostly linked to the exchange rate as were loans given by nonprofit institutions, mortgage banks and some other lenders. As a
matter of fact several years before the rather expected devaluation the alternative of linkage to the cost-of-living index had
been abolished and borrowers from the previously mentioned
sources had to link their debts to the exchange rate of the dollar.

The devaluation increased the value of the dollar in Israeli
Pounds by two thirds, and thus the nominal value of debts
linked to the exchange rate should have risen correspondingly.
Indeed as far as private loans to the public sector are concerned
this actually took place. But though most of the loans granted
by the government were long-term loans, the government had
to yield to the pressure groups involved. Borrowers whose loans
were linked to the exchange rate were given the choice of
either repaying the loans within a rather short period without
any linkage whatsoever, or switching to linkage to the cost-of-
living index, or sticking to their dollar-linkage. This arrangement, originated by the government, was extended half a year
later to the mortgage banks. Shortly afterwards linkage to the
rate of exchange was forbidden. Cf. *Bank of Israel Annual
Report, 1962* (Jerusalem, Israel, 1963), pp. 115-17 and 439-42.

It should also be noted that the large amounts of privately
held foreign-exchange bank deposits converted into Israeli
Pounds has been one of the major causes of the only partial
success of this devaluation.

of the value of their savings in terms of man-hours of work, thus enabling them to participate in the gains from productivity increases, to force them to share in cuts in available resources, and to contribute to price stability by having labor realize that any wage increase automatically increases the income of bond-holders as well. Such an index, however, cannot be applied generally; certainly it cannot be used to protect wage-earners themselves. Moreover, it is not clear that savers should participate in the benefits from rises in productivity as a matter of right. In some countries, such systems of linkage have quite possibly damaged the very idea of constant-purchasing-power bonds more than any other of their features.

It should be made clear, though, that devaluations under an inflation-proof economy will not be necessarily less efficient than they are in a "normal" economy. The purpose of devaluation is to promote exports and imports-substitutes industries; under full employment this may happen only at the expense of industries not directly related to international trade, and obviously such industries will not "permanently" decline unless local demand is cut. Whether devaluations will achieve a continuing effect in "normal" conditions is an open question, and it will remain so in an inflation-proof economy. If a devaluation is accompanied by a strict monetary policy, the price level would hardly change—the prices of goods and services not traded internationally going down. In this case the mechanism for protection against inflation would not operate at all. To the extent that monetary conditions do allow some increases in the price level, victims would be compensated, at least partly, by private beneficiaries from inflation, like creditors. To the extent that monetary policy is permissive—and if fiscal policy did not substitute a socially-approved tax for the inflation tax intentionally "killed" by the scheme—

devaluation would not have much chance to be permanently effective. But, depending on the importance of the import components in the commodities and services represented in the "escalating index," and on the frequency of adjustments, it might take some time for the original change in relative prices brought about by the devaluation to be completely offset.

Often when the issue is raised, it is claimed that since a "general" price index is not under the control of any private borrower, these borrowers could not be expected to link their borrowing to such an index. And since, allegedly, only a government can issue bonds linked to such an index—so goes the argument— this is just another scheme to favor the public sector. All that a private borrower can do, it is implied, is to guarantee the value of the loans he gets in terms of the prices of his own products. Bonds linked to the price of particular commodities, like railway tickets, electricity, or cement, exist and may satisfy some specific demand,[20] but they are certainly inferior as hedges against inflation to bonds linked to a general price index. Moreover, producers with liabilities escalated to prices of their own products might tend to have prices which would be especially rigid. Since every price increase increases proportionally the value of their debts, many firms might often find themselves in an impasse. Now certainly neither price rigidity nor bankruptcies are a solution to inflation. As a matter of fact, when taxes and subsidies are brought into the picture, it is not even clear that it always pays for a producer to escalate loans to the *market* price of his own products rather than to the general price level. In any case the borrower is only one part to the transaction, and it is not self-explanatory why his interests should rule. It should not be so difficult for firms to conduct their borrowing as if inflation is not going to take place at all. Changes in the price level change the real terms of contracts; all that is suggested here is to undo the change.

Needless to say, the price index chosen for escalation will become a tool of great political importance. Changes in this index might well turn into news headlines, for indeed they are important news for everybody. Pressure groups will do their best to influence it, and both the executive and legislative branches will certainly have the means to change it. This is not to say that there is anything wrong with such developments. Surely the intention here is not to deprive the government of means of redistributing incomes. The legislative branch will remain completely autonomous in deciding how to finance expenditures. As already mentioned, there is no contradiction at all, even between an escalated economy and measures imposing taxes on increases in money payments which result from that very escalation. Such taxes, being explicit, reflect a social decision. And the main evil of inflation is not in its distributional effects on incomes and net worths, but in the lack of social-decision backing for such effects.

Since no economy is a closed economy, objections to the scheme might be based on balance-of-payments arguments. It has not been accepted as obvious that general escalation would necessarily increase the rate of inflation, but such a possibility is not being ruled out. If this did happen, or more exactly, if the effect of escalation on the rate of inflation were greater in one economy than in others, then adverse developments might indeed follow in the balance-of-trade of *that* economy. In the capital-payments sector of the balance-of-payments, there might be actual improvement over a nonescalated case: certainly there would be less incentive for capital flights abroad, for such short-run capital export is undertaken rationally only if the rate of devaluation is expected to exceed the internal rate of price increase (except for the separate case where capital moves in response to international differentials in the short-run rate of interest). In other words, capital flights might still take place, but not anymore as hedges against inflation. In spite of this, it is not denied here that escalation may, in some countries, make devaluations more frequent (and in other countries necessarily more rare). But, excluding elements of national prestige, devaluation should, under the new setting, cause much less difficulty than it does in the existing system.

It might be argued—and obviously I am trying to think for possible opponents—that it would be very difficult to determine the rate of return to be paid on inflation-proof bonds. But like any rate of return, it would be determined by supply and demand.

It might also be argued that stocks may be currently used to protect the value of savings against inflation. But even if this were true—and in many economies the performance of stocks in this respect has often been far from satisfactory—escalated bonds are certainly an improvement, at least for nonspeculative savers. Since inflation-proof bonds are to some extent substitutes for stocks, the demand for stocks would probably be reduced. To the extent that profit-receivers have been benefiting from inflation, escalation would reduce the rate of profits, and thus produce another factor reducing the demand for stocks. I do not wish to discuss here the question of whether widespread ownership of equity is good or bad; it has important advantages in prosperity, but may have symmetrical disadvantages in case of an economic catastrophe. In addition, it is certainly as important for democratic capitalism to have savers less worried and less disappointed, which, it is believed, the scheme would probably achieve.

ESCALATION AND ORDINARY TAXES

Needless to say, the plan does call for some changes in the administration of ordinary taxes. Unless explicitly changed by the legislative body, income tax rates would now apply to income brackets stated in the currency of a given date which could be easily "translated" into new "figures." All tax payments would also be made in "constant-purchasing-power" currency, thus reducing the built-in flexibility of a progressive tax system. But, again, this in itself would not necessitate that depreciation be computed according to replacement costs, or that inventory profits (or losses) rising from changes in the price level be necessarily tax exempt. As for outlay taxes, the interests of the fiscus during escalated inflations, just as during ordinary ones, would be served by *ad valorem* taxes. It would be possible, of course, to use specific, but escalated, outlay taxes; but in practice this might be much clumsier.

On the other hand, it is to be expected that the use of outlay taxes will be much reduced in countries where escalated inflation is practiced, for whenever such taxes—with monetary support—raise the price level, taxpayers will get compensation, so that such taxes, like inflation itself, will become functionless. But certainly it makes no sense to protect everybody from indirect taxes just because they raise the price level. The very existence of government expenditures necessitates that the private sector give up resources, so that real compensation for all taxes is impossible. And it does not seem justifiable to compel the government to impose its taxes only directly on households.*

* Such a policy will usually be supported by labor unions. The ideal tax scheme from their point of view is a rather progressive system of taxes on income and wealth. There are obvious difficulties in a position which simultaneously supports

The same treatment would be given to changes in the local prices of imported goods and services due either to changes in the terms of trade or to the devaluation of currencies.

The very idea of the escalation is intended to prevent both the arbitrary inflation-induced transfers of income and net worths within the private sector, and the similarly arbitrary inflation tax. But there is no intention to frustrate the government by depriving it also of indirect taxes, (which, it has been argued, do not differ basically from direct taxes) and from the fruits of devaluations.

If the price level does rise, with monetary support, for reasons which are hardly connected with fiscal policy, it is important to compensate those who suffer by this price increase, so as to offset the inflation tax, and keep the agreed-upon income distribution unchanged. It is on these grounds that escalator clauses in wage contracts are justified, though under ordinary circumstances all they do is to shift the burden to the remaining defenseless sectors. When taxes are imposed, however, there is a social decision to reduce some or all disposable incomes and usually also to change the distribution of incomes. Therefore it is suggested here that all taxes be excluded from the escalating index,† even if the increase in the market price level is smaller than the increase in taxes so that

---

income taxes "in general" but demands "compensations" for the income taxes paid by the members of one's organization. But because outlay taxes are often regressive—so that, on the whole, labor unions would like to see them disappear or at least lose in importance—there is no contradiction involved in their efforts to protect their members from the burdens of outlay taxes.

† It may be added that because the Laspeyre index, based on a fixed pattern of expenditures, is the natural index for a cost-of-living index, any partial tax, which will almost always have substitution effects, will be overly compensated for.

excluding the taxes would actually reduce the index of the price level at factor costs.

It would be a wholesome experience for all involved to realize that escalation does indeed work both ways. Again, the basic rationale for the exclusion of taxes from the escalating index is that escalator clauses in wage or similar contracts are intended to keep unchanged a distribution of disposable income agreed upon between the parties to the contract, and not to protect either party against letting the government reduce the levels of their disposable incomes. The absurdity of the compensation for taxes would become much clearer if compensations were asked for *all* taxes. With government expenditures exceeding the total income of those receiving fixed payments, that would become an obvious practical impossibility.

Truly, an exclusion of taxes from the price index used for escalation purposes is justified even when escalation is applied only to particular incomes and assets.[21] In this latter case, compensation of some sectors for the price-raising effects of taxes shifts the tax burden to the remaining sectors, which may be unjust when feasible, and, often, a practical impossibility.

The inflationary consequences of a rise in money wages following an increase in the price index used for escalating wages may, let us remember, be easily underestimated. If the share of labor costs in the total expenses of an average firm is 50 per cent, it may be wrongly argued, a 20 per cent raise in money wages will increase its total costs by 10 per cent, and the prices of its products accordingly. Within a few additional steps, it seems to follow, additional effects on the price level through escalator clauses in wage contracts would become negligible. But this certainly cannot apply to the economy as a whole. If the wage increase is universal, as it is in the case of general adjustments of wages to changes in the escalating index, prices of all domestic materials used in production will also rise, sooner or later, to the same extent. With marginal-costs pricing—and if marginal costs include only labor and domestic materials—the increase in the price level will ultimately equal percentage-wise the original wage increase. Surely, long before the first wage increase achieves its end-result, wages would have been increased again and again following the rises in the escalating index. In practice, some elements of costs, like imported inputs, taxes and user costs, may rise proportionally less, and, with other pricing methods, fixed costs may also have a moderating effect on the price level. Yet user costs will also rise, for they are influenced by price expectations and the rise in wages will increase the rate of use and of depreciation of existing machines which thus will have to be replaced at an earlier date. As to imported inputs, their prices in a free-exchange economy will rise similarly to those of domestic inputs; while this is not true if the exchange rate is fixed by the authorities—so that import prices rise far less, if at all—this is only because the very level of the fixed exchange rate signifies in inflations a growing subsidy to imports.

Certainly, the very idea presented here is not original. All that it adds to previous proposals is the suggestion that escalation be general. Yet when presented to economists, businessmen, and politicians, reactions to it have been at best tolerant, rarely enthusiastic, probably because I have omitted some basic economic factors. But if the factors omitted are not economic but rather social-psychological—if, say, changes in the value of a unit of money are demoralizing even when nobody is economically hurt—then most of the economic literature on anti-inflationary policy has been completely misdirected.

Let me repeat, though, that attempts to sterilize inflation do not throw doubt on the national currency as a unit of value; it is inflation itself that does so. Objections to index loans or escalated wages on the grounds of the prestige of the national currency seem to me hypocritical. Such measures are needed only when there is no longer much confidence in the national currency. But that they are then needed is surely obvious. Similarly, as in the case of ordinary insurance of life or capital, most people would be ready to pay a premium for insurance against the risks of inflation and still be happy were those risks never realized.

NOTES

1. Cf. G. L. Bach, "The Impact of Moderate Inflation on Incomes and Assets of Economic Groups," *Federal Tax Policy for Economic Growth and Stability* (Washington, D.C.: Government Printing Office, 1956), pp. 71-82.

2. "Inflation has been defined by some writers as a tax. But the characteristic of this tax is that, at the same time as the state is taking part of the national income itself, it imposes on some classes of society a levy in favour of other classes." (C. Bresciani-Turroni, *The Economics of Inflation* (London: Allen & Unwin, 1937), p. 196.

3. Cf. G. L. Bach, "Monetary-Fiscal Policy Reconsidered," *Journal of Political Economy* (October 1949), reprinted in *Readings in Fiscal Policy*, selected by Arthur Smithies and J. Keith Butters (Homewood, Illinois: Richard O. Irwin, 1955), pp. 248-64, esp. 253-55.

4. See *Inflation*, ed. by D. C. Hague (London: Macmillan, 1962), especially the opinions of the late Erik Lindahl and Arthur W. Marget. There is much to be said in favor of J.C.R. Dow's remarks (summarized on p. 397)

against Lindahl's stress on price stability as the overriding aim of financial policy.

5. Cf. E. J. Mishan and L. A. Dicks-Mineaux, "Progressive Taxation in an Inflationary Economy," *The American Economic Review*, Vol. XLVIII (September 1958), pp. 590-606.

6. Milton Friedman, "Discussion of the Inflationary Gap," reprinted in *Essays in Positive Economics* (Chicago: University of Chicago Press, 1953), pp. 251-62.

7. Cf. the different approach of Ralph Turvey, "Inflation as a Tax in World War II," *The Journal of Political Economy*, Vol. LXIX (February 1961), pp. 70-73.

8. See Philip Cagan, "The Monetary Dynamics of Hyperinflation," in *Studies in the Quantity Theory of Money*, ed. by Milton Friedman (Chicago: University of Chicago Press, 1956), pp. 25-117, and esp. p. 78. Cagan rightly states that inflation, as a tax, may be appealing to legislators because it does not require detailed—or any—legislation. But his conclusion—that it is very easy to administer because all that is required is to spend newly-printed notes —may be entirely wrong if the printing of the new notes add little to the resources available for government use. Inflation may release resources from private consumption if it redistributes incomes in such a way as to promote savings, or if other variables that affect savings, including real balances, are affected by it in a way that increases savings. Resources for government use may be released by inflation if the increased savings, when forthcoming, are not completely offset by increased private investments. But whether these two-stage developments do occur or not is not self-evident.

9. See T. V. Houser, *The Cruelest Tax*, CED (1958), pp. 1-23, esp. p. 1.

10. Paul A. Samuelson and Robert M. Solow, "Analytical Aspects of Anti-Inflation Policy," *Papers and Proceedings of the American Economic Association, American Economic Review*, Vol. L, No. 2 (May 1960), pp. 177-94.

11. Abba P. Lerner, "Discussion," *Papers and Proceedings of the American Economic Association, American Economic Review*, Vol. L, No. 2 (May 1960), p. 215.

12. Discussed, for example, by Ursula K. Hicks in *Public Finance* (New York: Pitman, 1948), pp. 167-72. Arnold C. Harberger has made several unpublished calculations of the "excise tax" effect of several taxes.

13. Cf. Martin J. Bailey, "The Welfare Cost of Inflationary Finance," *The Journal of Political Economy*, Vol. LXIV (April 1956), pp. 93-110.

14. Jørgen Pedersen, "Wage Fixing According to the Price Index," *International Economic Papers*, Vol. 4 (1954), pp. 70-108, esp. pp. 85-92.

15. United Nations, Economic Commission for Latin America, "Index Clauses in Deferred Payments," *Economic Bulletin for Latin America* (October 1957), pp. 73-75; D. Finch, "Purchasing Power Guarantees for Deferred Payments," *Staff Papers*, International Monetary Fund, Vol. V (February 1956), pp. 1-22; John Hein, "A Note on the Use of Index Clauses Abroad," *Journal of Finance*, Vol. XV (December 1960), pp. 546-52; Guy Arvidsson, "Should We Have Index-Loans?" in *Inflation, op. cit.*, pp. 112-26. Arvidsson mentions Professor Palander's pioneering work on index loans, *Värdebestandighet, ett problem vid sparande, livförsäkringar och pensioner* (Uppsala, Sweden: 1957), which I did not read.

16. See C. Bresciani-Turroni, "Working of the Sliding Scale Applied to Wages in Italy," *Review of the Economic Conditions in Italy*, Vol. X (November 1956), Banca di Roma, pp. 519-47.

17. See D. Finch, *op. cit.*, p. 2.

18. See, for example, Peter Robson, "Index-Linked Bonds," *Review of Economic Studies*, Vol. XXVIII (October 1960), pp. 57-68; and A. Rubner, "The Abdication of the Israeli Pound as a Standard of Measurement for Medium and Long-Term Contracts," in the same issue, pp. 69-75; for a more unsympathetic attitude, see "Creep-

ing Inflation," Federal Reserve Bank of New York, *Monthly Review* (June 1959), pp. 86-94. In his article, "Should We Have Index Loans?" Guy Arvidsson mentions the negative attitude "both in their pronouncements and in practice" of the Directors of the Central Bank in Sweden (Riksbank) and of the National Debt Directors towards index loans. See *Inflation, op. cit.*, pp. 114-15.

19. See Sir Dennis H. Robertson, "Creeping Inflation," in *Economic Commentaries* (London, 1956), p. 124, fn.

20. See John Hein, *op. cit.*, and United Nations, Economic Commission for Latin America, "Index Clauses in Deferred Payments," *Economic Bulletin for Latin America* (October 1957), pp. 73-76.

21. Cf. Amotz Morag, "Escalator Clauses and Indirect Taxes," *The Indian Economic Journal*, Vol. III (October 1955), pp. 154-67.

INDEX

Ability to pay, 78-9
Accelerated depreciation, 80-1
Arvidsoon, Guy, 175, 176
Aujac, Henry, 45
Axelson, C. E., 139-40

Bach, G. L., 173
Bagehot, Walter, 157
Bailey, Martin, 175
Balanced-budget multiplier, 33
Bator, Francis, 17n.
Baumol, W. J., 44
Becker, Gary S., 44
Benefit-principle, 116
Blum, Walter J., 91, 92
Boulding, Kenneth E., 112
Bowman, Mary Jean, 91
Break, G. F., 32, 44, 48, 52, 70, 111
Bresciani-Turroni, C., 45, 173, 175
Bronfenbrenner, M., 45, 140
Brown, A. J., 140
Brown, H. G., 32
Buchanan, James A., 92, 140

Butters, J. Keith, 173

Cagan, Philip, 152n., 174
Cannan, Edwin, 105, 112
Capital formation, 29, 77
Capital-gains tax, 84, 85, 133, 137, 138
Capital stock, 77
Cary Brown, E., 62, 63, 64, 65, 66, 67, 71, 72, 103, 112
Chandler, Lester, 44
Chang, Ching Gwan, 64, 72
Chase, Sam B., 103
Clark, Colin, 3, 12, 13, 22, 146
Colwyn Committee, 39
Constant-purchasing-power bonds, 154-9
Consumption function, 64, 65, 66
Corporate income tax, 42
Cost-of-living index, 37, 68, 154-8, 162
Custom duties, on economic rent, 86

Defict financing, 8, 13, 14, 149-53

De Viti de Marco, Antonio, 92
Dicks-Mineau, L. A., 174
Direct taxes, 115-16
Domar, Evsey, 103, 104, 105, 106, 107, 110, 112
Douglas, Monteath, 22
Dow, J. C. R., 173
Downs, Anthony, 121, 140

Eckstein, Otto, 78
Economic efficiency of taxes, 47-57, 69
Economic growth, 78
Edgeworth, F. Y., 17, 23
Equal sacrifice approach to taxation, 73
Equality, 74
Equi-proportionate sacrifice, 73
Equi-revenue taxes, 59
Escalation: of bank deposits and bonds, 158-9; Israeli experience in, 164n.; and ordinary taxes, 170-3; to the price of gold or foreign exchange, 162, 163; to the prices of specific products, 166; of wages to a c.o.l. index, 37; of wages to a wage index, 164-5
Estate taxes, 133, 137
Excess-burden of a partial tax, 49-52
"Excise-tax" effect, 67, 111
Expense accounts, 134-5

Fellner, William J., 14, 23
Ferber, Robert, 139
Finch, D., 157, 175
Fiscal policy, 47
Fiscal psychology, 88-90, 115-30
Fisher, Irving, 157
Friedman, Milton, 52, 72, 106, 112, 113, 147, 148, 157, 159, 174
Fringe benefits, 134-5
Functional-finance, 6, 19, 46

Galbraith, John Kennedy, 129, 140
Gilbert, J. C., 41
Goode, Richard, 23, 32, 44, 71, 72, 111, 145n.
Gopal, M. H., 92
Government: expenditures, optimal size of, 7; as a fair partner, 102; public relation of, 95
Grünfeld, Yehuda, 112

Hague, D. C., 173
Hall, Challis A., 105, 110, 112
Hansen, Alvin H., 112
Hansen, Bent, 26, 27, 44
Harberger, Arnold C., 23, 111, 112, 175
Haroé, Yoram, 81n.
Harris, Seymour E., 140
Hein, John, 175, 176
Hicks, J. R., 34, 44, 45, 92
Hicks, U. K., 92, 115, 139, 175
Hirshleifer, Jack, 78
Houser, T. V., 154, 174

Income distribution, 20, 74-9, 135-6, 143
Income tax: advantages of a proportional, 132-3; base, 18, 19, 25, 85-9; as concealed sales tax, 41; shifting, attempted shifting and incidence of, 38-43; sur-tax, 138; withholding in, 118, 129; yield of a progressive, 84
Indirect taxes, 26, 37, 49, 89, 115, 116; as "excess

profit taxes," 90; flexibility of, 89; and morals, 87-91

Indirectness in taxation, 125-6

Inflation, 142-76; allocational effects of, 156; beneficiaries of, 161; characteristics of, 145, 146; cost push, 160; deflationary effects of, 148, 159; and devaluation, 162-8; distributional effects of, 143; employment loss resulting from fear of, 154-5; evils of, 145, 146; functionless, 150; incidence of, 151; monetary character of, 147; psychological causes of, 124-6; repressed, 85

Inflation tax, 142-54; base of, 147; measurements of, 148-53

Inflationary gap, 146-67

Inheritance taxes, 133, 137

Interest, rate of, 30-1, 61-3

Investments, effects of taxation on, 68, 76, 77, 98-102

Ito, Hanya, 132, 141

Jevons, W. Stanley, 157

Joseph, M. F. W., 52, 70

Kahn, Harry C., 141

Kaldor, Nicholas, 47, 48, 61, 68, 70, 71

Kalven, Harry, Jr., 91, 92

Katona, George, 123, 140

Keynes, J. M., 91, 92, 119

Klein, John, 153

Kuh, Edwin, 112

Kurihara, Kenneth K., 45, 140

Kuznets, Simon, 7, 22

Labor standard, 36

Labor supply, effects of taxation on, 96-8

Labor unions, 36-7, 122

Lerner, Abba P., 6, 22, 45, 70, 154, 175

Lindahl, Erik, 173, 174

Little, I. M. D., 52

Liu, Ta-Chung, 64, 72

Loss-offsets, 36, 101, 103

Lubell, H., 71

McCall, John J., 44, 45

Machlup, Fritz, 157

Marget, Arthur W., 173

Markowitz, Harry, 106, 113

Marshall, Alfred, 157

Mayer, Thomas, 22

Means, Gardiner C., 64, 72

Meyer, John R., 112

Millikan, Max F., 70

Minimum sacrifice approach to taxation, 73

Mishan, E. J., 174

Money balances, 30, 33-5, 52-4; demand of business and households for, 33-5, 54-5, 66; escalated to a cost of living index, 158-61

Money illusion, 47, 59, 63-8, 118-20; sociological explanations of, 120-4

Morag, Amotz, 45, 176

Multiple level sales taxes, 130

Musgrave, Richard A., 21, 23, 35, 43, 44, 70, 71, 92, 103, 105, 106, 107, 110, 111, 112, 130, 131, 135, 136n., 139, 140, 141

Net-worth tax, 138

Niemeyer, Otto, 157

Ojha, P. D., 22

Olds, James, 140

Painter, Mary S., 71
Palander, Tord, 175
Palgrave, H. H. Inglis, 112
Parsons, Talcott, 122, 140
Patinkin, Don, 30, 44, 70
Pechman, Joseph A., 22, 92
Pedersen, Jørgen, 45, 164, 175
Petty, Mary, 45
Pigou, A. C., 15, 23
Poll tax, 17
Price rigidity, 32, 166
Progression, 84, 87-8
Progressive taxation, 60, 73-93; and economic distortions, 85-6; and "equi-distributional fiscal sets," 81; and excess profits tax, 83; exemption of imputed rent, 81; exemption from income tax of interest on state or local bond, 80; and partial progressivity, 79-82; and percentage depletion, 80; and "Planned Inflation," 87; and spurious progressivity, 82, 83
Propensity to consume and/or to spend, 60-6
Psychic income, 18, 85
Psychological cost of paying taxes, 13, 14, 21, 95, 116-18, 127-8, 139

Quantity Theory of Money, 27-33, 41

Real-balance effect, 30-1, 55, 63, 148-9
Real money balances, 30-1, 63, 148, 153n.
Regressivity in taxation, 59, 60, 80
Rehn, Gosta, 45

Risk, 104, 105
Risk taking, effects of taxation on, 103-10
Ritter, Lawrence S., 64, 72
Robertson, Sir Dennis H., 176
Robson, Peter, 175
Rolph, Earl R., 23, 32, 52, 70, 71, 72, 103, 104, 112
Rostas, C., 92
Rubner, A., 175

Samuelson, Paul, 77, 92, 99, 111, 154, 174
Savage, L. J., 106, 112, 113
Savings, 49, 61, 62, 68, 98-103, 134; effects of taxation on, 99-100; purposes of, 55-6
Schmölders, G., 140
Seers, Dudley, 91
Shifting and attempted shifting of taxes, 35-43
Shils, Edward A., 140
Shoup, Carl, 47, 48, 70, 115, 131n., 132, 139, 141
Simons, Henry, 71, 73, 74, 91
Slichter, Sumner, 157
Smith, Dan Throop, 22
Smithies, Arthur, 71, 173
Social costs of public expenditures, 7
Social costs of public revenues, 7, 14
Solow, R., 154, 174
Stigler, George S., 112
Streeten, Paul, 104, 113
Subjective burden, 54

Tax credits and tax exemptions, 80-1
Taxes: administration, 19, 88-90; allocational effects of, 15-18, 21, 56, 59, 67-69, 76-7, 94-112; base, 25, 96; deflationary effects of,

46-71; direct, 26, 37, 49, 89, 115, 116; distributional effects of, 15-18, 73-93; on economic surplus, 110; effects on investments, 98-102; effects on labor supply, 96-8; effects on risk taking, 103-10; general, 25, 39-40, 57, 95; indirect, 26-30, 59; limits of, 3-21; partial, 25, 35, 39-41, 49-53, 57, 60, 67, 96, 100, 115; and the price level, 8, 26-45; purchasing-power effects of, 127
Thin, Thun, 92
Tobin, James, 70, 103, 105, 110, 113, 140

Trescott, Paul B., 70, 111
Turvey, Ralph, 45, 72, 174

Utility function, 105-9

Value-added tax, 127-39; a progressive, 136-7
Velocity of money, transactions, 27-9, 33-4, 63, 66
Visine, François, 22

Wage index, 164
Wage standard, 36
Walker, David, 70
White, William H., 71, 72
Woytinski, E. S., 111
Woytinski, W. S., 111

Young, Allyn A., 91

Studies in Economics

Trade Unions in the Age of Affluence. William H. Miernyk (SE 1)

Higher Education in the American Economy. André Danière (SE 2)

The Italian South: Economic Development in Mediterranean Europe. Gustav Schachter (SE 3)

Welfare Economics: Seven Introductory Essays. Edward Mishan (SE 4)

On Taxes and Inflation. Amotz Morag (SE 5)

Economic Liberalism, Vol. I: *The Beginnings.* William D. Grampp (SE 6)

Economic Liberalism, Vol. II: *The Classical View.* William D. Grampp (SE 7)

Rich and Poor Lands: The Widening Gap. L. J. Zimmerman (SE 8)